A GUIDE TO
COMPUTER LITERATURE

A GUIDE TO
COMPUTER LITERATURE

*An introductory survey of the
sources of information*

SECOND EDITION, REVISED AND EXPANDED

ALAN PRITCHARD
ALA AI Inf Sc

LINNET BOOKS & CLIVE BINGLEY

FIRST PUBLISHED 1969

SECOND EDITION REVISED AND EXPANDED
FIRST PUBLISHED 1972 BY CLIVE BINGLEY LTD
AND SIMULTANEOUSLY PUBLISHED IN THE USA
BY LINNET BOOKS, AN IMPRINT OF
SHOE STRING PRESS INC,
995 SHERMAN AVENUE, HAMDEN, CONNECTICUT 06514
PRINTED IN GREAT BRITAIN
0–208–01182–X

CONTENTS

PREFACE TO THE SECOND EDITION

THE FIRST EDITION of this book incorporated developments in the field of computer information up to the summer and autumn of 1968. The short space of four years since then has seen such an increase in the amount of information and in secondary and tertiary information sources that this second edition is necessary. A measure of the growth of computer information is the number of periodical titles in computing, which seems to be doubling every 4-6 years, as compared with the doubling period of 10-15 years which is generally quoted for science and technology as a whole.

In addition there has been an increasing awareness of the value of and need for computer information in both the computing and library professions. Examples from computing are the steady growth of the National Computing Centre's information services, which were more or less non-existent in 1967-1968, and the series of international seminars held by IAG on the ' Not invented here ' complex. The library world, too with the formation of the Aslib Computer Information Group (entirely distinct from the Computer Applications Group) which has been very active with meetings and working parties, has realised that the problems of computer information are sufficiently complex and unique to be studied in depth.

This edition differs from the first in the following ways:

1 The reorganisation of many chapters (eg on periodicals, data books and directories) to provide a more helpful arrangement in view of the increased amount of information included.

2 The addition of chapters on particular problem areas such as software and hardware.

7

3 More detailed bibliometric data resulting from the completion of the research project at the North-Western (now North London) Polytechnic School of Librarianship. Whilst this data relates to computer literature published in 1966, and is therefore out of date in some respects, it does provide a first approximation to an understanding of the information transfer process. It is to be hoped that others will carry out further similar studies so that we can have a better understanding of the changes with time of the information transfer process.

4 The value of the individual forms of material can only be fully understood within the context of a generalised theory of information transfer, which looks at the process flow from originator to user via formal and informal sources of information and information centres. A theoretical understanding can then lead to more effective action to improve the process. Included, therefore, are some general comments on information transfer and specific comments on the place of each form. It is hoped that these will be useful to the library profession at large.

5 Some material has, of course, been deleted in order to concentrate upon more recently published items. This does not, in any way deny the continuing usefulness of many older works and the first edition may continue to be consulted for information about them.

Finally, acknowledgements are due to the National Computing Centre Ltd, where I am employed, for permission to undertake this revision (all my comments are made in a purely private capacity, and in no way reflect the official policy of NCC), and to all colleagues who have made helpful suggestions for improving the book.

ALAN PRITCHARD

PREFACE

THIS BOOK WAS initially written as an exercise for the electrical and electronic engineering paper of the Library Association final examination (list C) at the North-Western Polytechnic School of Librarianship. The carrying out of a research project on the statistical analysis of computer literature, sponsored by the Office of Scientific and Technical Information (who of course bear no responsibility for the statements in this book), provided an opportunity for an even closer look at the computer literature. Consequently, this provided a unique opportunity to recast the original exercise into book form.

Numerical data on the literature has come from two reports. One is an interim report presenting results based on an incomplete data base, but which nevertheless has provided a useful indication of the literature. This report is A Pritchard: *Statistical analysis of bibliographic structure: interim report* (North-Western Polytechnic, School of Librarianship, July 1968 (SABS-3)). The other report is an American one which has concentrated on the major abstracting services, P R Bagley: *Counting the number of documents published in 1966 in the field of information science and technology* (AFIPS 1968). Both projects are continuing and further reports will be issued.

The layout of this book is such that each chapter deals with a different form of material, starting with 'primary' forms (*ie* those that report original research work), followed by 'secondary' forms (*eg* abstracts, bibliographies etc), and finally ending with some miscellaneous types of material, and libraries.

The basic aim of the book is to describe these various forms of material in which computer literature appears. Important items are described and evaluated, except for individual mono-

9

graphic works such as books, theses, research reports etc. The reason for this is that there are so many books published which are all of about the same standard that it would be invidious to name only one or two of them. Many booklists exist, *eg* for courses in the field, which, with *Computing reviews,* will provide recommended works in any branch of computer science.

My thanks are due to the following: OSTI, who sponsored the project which has given me the opportunity to study the literature; to the North-Western Polytechnic School of Librarianship, which has housed the project; to the staff of both these organisations for their helpful comments; to HERTIS for leave of absence to carry out the project; to the librarian and staff of the Netherlands Automatic Information Processing Research Center; to the librarian and staff of City University, London; to the librarians of many computer and other libraries in the London area and elsewhere; and to AFIPS for permission to quote extensively from their report.

1 COMPUTER LITERATURE

ONE OF THE MOST important problems facing all scientists, technologists and managers today is keeping up with the vast amount of literature poured out on all sides.

The information contained in this literature is important and enables the reader to remain well informed after a period of formal training; to answer specific enquiries; to be stimulated by new ideas; and vastly to extend the circle of people upon whose experience he can draw.

The problem however is the size of this literature. About 30,000 to 35,000 scientific and technical journals are published throughout the world—producing some one to two million papers. In addition there are books, conference proceedings, standards, patents, trade literature and, that peculiarity of the postwar world, research reports—all of which the scientist must be aware of, if he is to keep up with developments in his own field.

Computer literature contributes about 40,000-50,000 items per year, and it is estimated that this is now growing at least by ten per cent per year. The size of the problem is not yet therefore overwhelming (as, for example, chemistry is becoming, with well over 300,000 abstracts published each year in *Chemical Abstracts,* and its five millionth abstract published in 1971). It is serious enough, however, because of the nature of computers themselves, and the extraordinary lack of interest shown by the computing profession in its own information problems.

Computer science and technology is a service or tool technology. Whilst there is a body of theory and practice relating to computers as such, the prime purpose of computers is to service other technologies and disciplines. This means that the literature is produced by two distinct groups of people: by computer scientists and engineers, and by the users of computers.

It means, in terms of literature output, that, not only will there be 'core' material appearing in computer journals or aimed at computer professionals, but that items on computers will appear in the literature of all other subjects where computers are applied. The parallels between computer literature and documentation literature (another service technology) are very strong.

A quantitative measure of this feature is the degree of scatter of the literature. In any subject a large proportion of the periodical literature will be published in relatively few journals, whilst the remainder will be published in a succession of less relevant journals. This concept was first formulated mathematically by S C Bradford[2] and has since been refined. It is known as Bradford's Law of Scattering and has analogs in many other fields of human activity, *eg* linguistics (as Zipf's Law), economics (Pareto's Law), business and industry (the 80-20 Rule) and computing (where it is the basis for the pushdown stack).

	% references		
% of journals in	*25*	*50*	*75*
Physics abstracts 1961	1·73	4·7	11·8
British journals 1963/64	0·51	1·9	7·8
Physics abstracts 1964	1·52	5·7	17·0
Physics abstracts 1965	1·42	4·85	12·1
Chemistry	0·81	2·8	9·7
Bio-chemistry	0·35	1·4	6·6
Petroleum	0·9	2·9	10·7
Physikalische berichte	1·34	4·43	11·4
Bulletin signaletique	0·79	4·14	13·8

TABLE 1 : Distribution of references

Sample data from a variety of studies are presented in table 1. The comparable data for computing for 25%, 50% and 75%

of references are 2%, 6·7%, and 20·4% respectively. We can immediately see from this that, whilst the percentage of core journals is much the same as that in other disciplines, the high figure for 75% coverage of references means that the literature is very much more scattered than that of other disciplines. This fact has important implications for the abstracting of computer literature, which will be discussed in chapter 13.

The figure of 6·7 % given in the previous paragraph represents a total of 107 journals and a list of these appears as appendix 1 (page 177).

BIBLIOMETRIC PROPERTIES OF THE LITERATURE
Intuitive knowledge of the literature is not enough. In order to make rational decisions at any stage of information transfer we must be able to describe the bibliometric properties of the literature, at least reasonably precisely. This section presents some basic general bibliometric properties—those relating to specific forms appear in the relevant chapters.

Country of publication: The countries contributing more than 1% to the literature are: United States (53%), USSR (14·2%), United Kingdom (8·15%), West Germany (5·5%), Japan (3·85%), France (2·95%), Czechoslovakia (1·5%), East Germany (1·5%) and Holland (1·38%). 33 other countries contributed the remaining 7·5%.

Language of publication: Languages contributing more than 1% to the literature are: English (66·5%), Russian (14·4%), German (7·25%), Japanese (3·45%), French (3·175%) and Czech (1·22%). 19 other languages contributed the remaining 4·05%.

Forms of publication: The major internal form was the journal-type paper (95%). Surprisingly, however, printed program listings contributed as much as 3·25% to the literature.

Author affiliations: The main types of author affiliations were: firms (49·5%), universities (27·2%), other research organisations (13·9%), government (5·52%), and armed services (3·86%).

13

Publishers: The main publishers of ' separates ' (*ie* anything except journal articles) were: government (40·9%), firms (24·9%), universities (16·2%), research organisations (11·2%), armed services (4·76%) and societies (1·28%).

HARD SCIENCE / SOFT SCIENCE?

Derek J de Solla Price has, for many years, attempted to use bibliometrics to illuminate the history and sociology of science. In a recent publication[1] he has used two measures to determine whether a discipline can be called a ' hard ' science, a ' soft ' science, a technology or a non-science. These two measures were (a) the number of references per article and (b) the percentage of references to literature of the last five years. Table 2 shows the results of investigating over 200 journals.

	lower quartile	median	upper quartile
reference/article	10	16	22
% in last 5 years	21	32	42

TABLE 2 : Summary of 200 journals

The implications of this table as stated by Price are :

a) In terms of references per article the scholarship norm is 10-22 references. If a discipline falls below this, it tends to rely on *ex cathedra* pronouncements, with the implication that culminating scholarship does not exist, it exists but is irrelevant, it exists relevantly but is unknown, or is a technology. A possible fifth alternative is that it is a young science.

b) In terms of the five year percentage, a figure greater than the upper quartile indicates a hard science. If the figure is greater than 60%, then competition is the fashion and ' invisible colleges ' (see Price's *Little science, big science*) are greatly in existence.

The implication for information transfer is that citation indexes should be used together with the social engineering of the invisible colleges. If the index is below the lower quartile then the discipline is ' humanistic ', in that existing knowledge is digested, matured and comes forth as new words of wisdom. One of the implications is the greater value of archival libraries.

	number of articles	refs / article	per cent in last five years
Commun ACM	27	7	69
	27	8	72
	30	7	77
	35	6	70
	18	11	70
Computer J	19	5	52
IEEE Trans Comp	25	8	42
Journal ACM	14	8	31

TABLE 3 : Computer journal data

Table 3 shows the results for the computer journals studied by Price. These figures present a most interesting paradox. Intuitively one would say that the latter three journals are the ones which conform most closely to the pattern of academic journals in the physical sciences, and yet it is these which have the lowest figures for the 5 year percentage. The explanation for this is not immediately apparent and more work needs to be done here.

Computing is both a young science and one in which there is little awareness of the value of information. One would expect, therefore, the figures for the number of references per article to be low, as indeed they are. Only a continuous monitoring of this parameter will indicate whether this is changing with time.

REFERENCES

1 Price, D J de Solla: Citation measures of hard science, soft science, technology and nonscience. *In*: Nelson, C E *and* Pollock, D K (eds) *Communications among scientists and engineers.* D C Heath, 1970, pp 3-22.

2 Bradford, S C *Documentation.* 1948; 2nd edition, 1953. Chapter 9 : The documentary chaos.

2 THE COST OF INFORMATION IN COMPUTING

THE MOST PRESSING problem facing the information world today is to provide sound economic justification to management for the support of libraries and information units, and to government for the support of national information plans.

It is not enough to claim that, in general, information is a ' good thing '. Management must be shown that information services contribute directly to profits, and hence to the survival of the firm, in precisely the same way that a manufacturing plant does. Governments must be shown that information at both a local and national level is essential for a healthy national economy.

Whilst it is easy to state these objectives, the difficulty lies in carrying them out, and it is possible that in the long run the techniques of cost-benefit analysis will be able to help the information world. Occasionally one is able to quantify very precisely the benefit of a piece of information when, for example, a research worker comes back and says ' If I had not been given this information, I would have spent £x thousand on research '.

Most information workers come across examples like this in the course of their work, and it is to be regretted that the Library Association or Aslib are not systematically collecting case histories of this type. Examples of the reverse situation are also well known; that is, where a failure to use information already in existence has wasted money. There are many recorded examples of this, and they are often quoted in connection with the ' language barrier ' and the need for translations—especially from Russian to English. Even more, they can be quoted as examples of the need to *read* translations and not to be put off by the sometimes odd terminology and phraseology. There have been well documented cases where information has been translated from Russian to English and still not used. In consequence a great deal of money has been wasted.

Although not related to the language barrier, the following is a classic example which was reported in a major chemical periodical.[1] A failure to read the literature on titanium stress corrosion cost the US space program more than $1.5m. Pressure tests were carried out on twenty titanium fuel tanks using methanol. When two failed the tests, hurried investigations showed that methanol causes stress corrosion in titanium. This fact was reported in the literature ten years before, and again at the national conference of the National Association of Corrosion Engineers the previous April.

As well as this type of case study we can make a more theoretical estimate of the cost of research and development duplication through lack of information within the computer industry. In 1964, Martyn of Aslib reported on interviews with over 600 scientists.[2] He found that losses due to avoidable late discovery (that is, actual duplication of research, or information which would have saved time, money or research) were associated with 9% of projects. He made the assumption, therefore, that 10% of project expenditure might be saved, and hence that 0·9% of total expenditure on research might be saved. This was admittedly a crude measure and was believed to be too low for the following three reasons:

a) The figures only take account of complete duplication, and not projects in which information caused (or would have caused if it had been known of at the time) a change in the research plan. A change in plan also costs money.

b) The study only covered information which was actually discovered. There must have been items of information or evidence of duplication which were not discovered, and hence further loss would have been caused.

c) Finally, a figure of 10% ' wastage ' was assumed. In my opinion this is an extremely conservative estimate.

Martyn was investigating the cost of duplication in research generally in the United Kingdom—a cost which he puts at £6

17

million. The factors mentioned above would, it was thought, probably double this figure. The Director of Aslib however has suggested that the figure may be too low by a factor as great as five or even ten[5]. Thus a total loss figure of five to ten per cent is indicated. A study carried out at the BP Research Centre put the total loss at five per cent[5]. American sources quoted in the same reference reported that the annual cost to the US economy of duplication of scientific effort has been variously estimated at $200 million and $1,000 million, representing two and nine per cent respectively of the 1958/9 US research expenditure.

We can apply the same reasoning to the computer industry, since this figure covers not only research in the normal sense as carried out in universities and manufacturing firms, but also the process of systems analysis and design and programming which is carried out when implementing any computer application in a user organisation.

However the figure of wastage of 1% reported by Martyn must be revised in the light of the comments above and also because:

a) The work reported studied the hard sciences and, compared with other disciplines, the state of information awareness in computing is extremely low.

b) It is well known that a great deal of duplication occurs in the writing of applications programs and utility routine. This is the *raison d'etre* of NCC's National Computer Program Index and the various algorithm libraries such as *Collected algorithms from CACM,* and that at Queen's University, Belfast etc. A number of conferences have also been held on this topic by IFIP.

c) The balance of expenditure between hardware and software has shifted from that of 10 years ago when the relative costs were about 70 : 30 on hardware : software, to the present day when the situation is completely reversed. The major expenditure of any installation is now upon software in its most general sense.

In view of these factors, for the computer industry we can

assume that the figure of 5% is a very conservative estimate of wastage as a result of the lack of information.

The Hoskyns report[3] presents figures and estimates for the total expenditure on data processing in the UK for the period 1968-1980 as follows:

	£m
1968	427·3
1970	682·4
1975	1,583·0
1980	2,724·5

Whilst the projected figures for 1975 and 1980 must obviously be a matter of some debate, it is unlikely that they will prove to be grossly wrong.

Let us therefore apply to this forecast the figures of 1% and 5% wastage which has been previously derived.

	Wastage £m	
	1%	5%
1968	4·273	21·365
1970	6·824	34·12
1975	15·83	79·15
1980	27·245	136·225

Even these extraordinary figures underestimate the real situation, since they are based upon actual expenditures and do not take into account the fact that firms are increasingly using the computer as the cornerstone of their operations. Without the computer to provide management information; to control stocks, production, sales, accounting etc, a multi-million pound business may not be able to operate. The true value of the computer is thus not the annual or initial cost of hardware, software, personnel and consumables, but the whole turnover of the business concerned.

Returning, however, to the theme of the first paragraphs of this section, techniques must be developed for measuring the return on an investment in an information system. If we could

19

be certain that an information system would have cut wastage by one half—say at worst by only £3·4m in 1970—then an expenditure of perhaps £1m on that system would be far more profitable than most ventures. Until such principles come to gain general acceptance though, we can only point out the facts of wastage—at best £6·8m in 1970, rising to £27·2m in 1980, and more probably £34·1m rising to £136·2m.

Some evidence of the savings to be made from improved information service comes from the Information Exchange Group (IEG) experiment conducted by the US National Institutes of Health (NIH).

The seven (eventually) IEG's were designed to facilitate the rapid exchange of information between small groups of scientists with similar research interests. It was a formalisation of the 'invisible college' system, facilitating an enlargement of the normal college by the organisation of reproduction and mailing facilities for the research papers which it was desired to circulate.

At the end of the experiment, 3,662 scientists were involved. In response to a final questionnaire, 466 participants (ie approximately 13%) reported 1,111 instances in which advance information influenced their research decisions, and cited 346 instances in which such information prevented unnecessary duplication. They also provided quantitative estimates of time and money saved or lost as a result of IEG information. 421 reported instances led to an estimated total saving of 1,959 months and more than $500,000.[4]

The American Institute of Physics, in a report on a National Information System for Physics,[6] estimated that 2 hours per month of time saved per physicist by such a system would be a 'gross understatement'. The average must be several times as high as this conservative figure. It must be carefully noted that physics is a research-oriented 'hard' science with an enormously greater degree of information usage than the computer industry. It consequently has less scope for improvement. If 2 hours/month is a 'gross understatement' for physics, the figure for the computer industry must be at least five times greater.

20

However, so as not to overstate our case, let us assume that a national information plan for computers could save professional staff 2 hours/month, and let us define ' professional staff ' in this context as programmers and upwards, including (in the commercial field) sales consultants. Then, since there are about 40,000 professional staff in the UK, the total saving would be nearly one million man-hours per year. The total cash saving of one million man-hours per years is no less than £3,000,000. In view of the likely understatements, and the ignoring of the fact that a national plan will affect all who use computers (not only computer professionals), the true savings must be many times higher still. It offers in one year a greater return than the entire investment in a national plan for many years.

REFERENCES

1 *Chemical engineering* Dec 5 1966, 69.

2 Martyn, J : Unintentional duplication of research. *New scientist* Feb 6 1964, 338.

3 *UK computer industry trends 1970 to 1980.* Hoskyns Group Ltd, October 1969, 21p.

4 *Scientific and technical communication,* National Academy of Sciences, 1969, 322p.

5 Cole, P F and Brockis, J : How much information work? *New scientist* Oct 5 1967, 36.

6 *A program for a National Information System for Physics 1970-1972.* American Institute of Physics, August 1969. AIP-ID 69R.

3 PERIODICALS IN INFORMATION TRANSFER

THE FIRST scientific periodical—the *Philosophical Transactions of the Royal Society* was founded in 1665. The following three hundred years has seen a steady exponential growth, until today there cannot be less than 50,000 scientific and technical periodicals in existence.

There are at least 800 computer periodicals, and many thousands more which are of interest to the computer professional because of the application-oriented material that will appear in them. It is surely true to say that virtually every periodical in existence in whatever field (and this even includes the colour supplements of Sunday newspapers) will carry at least one article on computing in a period of, say, two to three years—so great is the penetration of computers into all aspects of society.

In spite of the post-war growth of the research report, the periodical is still the most important information transfer channel for primary information. Periodicals will often be the only information source used, and because of the references given will be a guide to information as well.

The importance of periodicals lies primarily in the fact that they are published regularly and frequently, and therefore will contain more up-to-date information than books. Additionally, articles, on specific topics are able to go into much greater depth regarding methodology, while articles on general topics can provide an overview in the space of a few pages. This latter facility is of great use to the busy manager who cannot spare the time to read a book.

There are a number of different types of periodical. Most writers on scientific information tend to take the stand that there is some sort of merit rating to be attached to each type of periodical, with the formal scientific journal reporting original research being in some way the 'best' or 'most important'. These writers have forgotten, however, that the *audience* of the journals must be considered, and the journal type which is 'best' for academically trained, postgraduate researchers is most definitely not the best for a manager attempting to understand the working of the machine which has upset all his previous systems and seems to be making him redundant.

In the discussion that follows, therefore, no statements are made about the relative merits of particular types of periodicals. The only judgement that can and should be made is whether a particular journal is reaching the right audience, and content is only one of the factors that determine this. As in all societies, there is a division of labour and some periodicals attempt to reach the academic world whilst others reach managers. Each has its own job to do and each could not function without the others.

We can classify periodicals in a variety of useful ways—by content (*eg* full papers or abstracts), by subject matter (*eg* programming or computer aided design), by level, by type of publisher or by country. For the purposes of the following chapters which discuss individual primary periodicals our first classification is by level. Within level the division is by country.

Three useful levels of primary periodicals can be distinguished and each plays an important role in information transfer: academic, commercial and news periodicals. Abstracting journals are secondary sources of information and are dealt with later in chapter 14.

Academic periodicals are those which report directly upon scientific research. They are edited at a scholarly level and the individual papers are refereed by members of the researcher's peer group. They consequently have a high prestige value and can be very selective in the papers published. On the whole they are published by societies and institutions in the field, although an increasing number is published by commercial publishers (*eg* Academic Press, Elsevier, Pergamon etc). As well as the major articles there may also be a section of short notes (as in *IEEE transactions on computers*) reporting on current work, letters to the editor, book reviews and society news. The tendency however is for societies to publish two journals—one at academic level and the other at commercial level. It is the latter which carries most society news and other service features (letters, reviews, advertisements etc). Examples are *Computer journal* and *Computer bulletin, IEEE transactions on computers* and *Computer, AEDS journal* and *AEDS monitor.*

Academic periodicals tend to be more aware of their responsibilities within the information transfer process. They will insist upon good abstracts and references being part of an article and the quality of these should be taken into account by the referees. In recent years they have been including keywords for indexing purposes as well. The two ACM periodicals, *IEEE transactions on computers, Software practice and experience* and *Information processing letters* all do this (among others), but the keywords are supplied on an *ad hoc* basis by the authors or editors. This, of course, rather nullifies the standardisation that this activity requires. It is a noteworthy fact that in all other disciplines where the publication of keywords is carried out, the construction of a standard thesaurus of descriptors has preceded publication of descriptors attached to articles. We have only to compare keywords published in the computer periodicals with those in chemical engineering to recognise the failure of the approach adopted by the computer periodicals. It is to be hoped that the NCC *Thesaurus of computing terms* will perform, for computing, a similar function to the *Thesaurus of engineering and scientific terms,* the *Chemical engineering thesaurus* (AIChE, 1961) or the *Thesaurus of pulp paper terms* (Institute of Paper Chemistry, 1969).

Commercial periodicals can be defined for our purposes as journals which are aimed roughly at the level of the working practitioner (*eg* programmer, systems analyst or engineer) or the well-informed manager. The articles will not be at the high research level of the academic group. They provide interpretations of basic research, and in fact form the main means by which the results of basic research are disseminated to working practitioners (whereas academic periodicals tend to talk only to other research workers). They also provide articles of general interest to their readers and will act as a buffer between computing and its users. In all of these tasks, especially the latter, they have a very important role to perform.

Commercial periodicals tend to have shorter articles and fewer of them, with a much higher percentage of service features, *ie* letters to the editor, advertisements, notes on new literature and products (both hardware and software), news of people and events, forthcoming events, coverage of the work of the leading societies and institutions, situations vacant and reader service cards. Within this group there is a continuous graduation from the more technical (such as *Computer design*) to those which are mainly news periodicals.

Commercial periodicals are not nearly as aware of their information transfer responsibilities as the journals in the first group, in spite of their key role. Articles tend not to have abstracts attached to them, they tend to be less well referenced (the majority are not referenced at all), and do not have keywords attached to them. Indexes to these journals are few and far between also. As their name implies, they are usually published by commercial publishers, although many are now published by societies to carry more general articles and society news.

News and special periodicals are those which deal mostly in much smaller units of information than the preceding two groups: news, market studies, reprints of press releases, or statistical data.

This type of periodical is usually of great value to an information service, as the latest news or market research data are of considerable interest to its clientele. Unfortunately their value is equalled only by the difficulty of handling the information contained in them. Techniques of abstracting and indexing which work well with the two previous groups fail with these periodicals, and no truly satisfactory solution has been found.

Possibly the solution would be for natural text-searching of the whole periodical on magnetic tape or disc (analogous to the technique employed in some legal information retrieval systems).

Special periodicals include not only those like *Computer survey* and *Computer characteristics review,* but also an increasing number of journals which are appearing in a non-printed format, such as braille or as audio tapes in cassette form. Librarians are going to encounter even more problems with these.

BIBLIOMETRIC PROPERTIES

There are well over 800 currently published computer periodicals. According to figures published in the *World list of computer periodicals* the total is growing at about 20% per year so that we can expect a doubling in the number of periodicals in about five years time.

Periodical articles form 37·6% of the total output of computer literature. This percentage comes mainly from the countries which produce the largest output of all forms of material, *ie* USA (43·4%) USSR (14·0%), UK (9·7%), West Germany (8·3%), Japan (4·6%) and France (3·4%), with Czechoslovakia, East Germany, Holland, Hungary, Italy, Poland and Rumania being other countries contributing more than 1% each to the periodical literature.

It is of interest to note, however, the percentage of a countries' output of computer literature which periodical articles comprise. For the major countries listed above this is: USA (37·9%), USSR (45·6%), UK (55·0%), West Germany (70·4%), Japan (55·5%) and France (52·8%). The low figure for the United States reflects the very high production and excellent bibliographic control of research reports whilst the high figure for West Germany reflects the relatively low output of both research reports and patents. The USSR tends to rely less upon periodicals and somewhat more upon collections of papers gathered together into books.

The mean length of a journal paper was 8·0 pages, and the

typical journal paper was abstracted 1·6 times. This latter figure is about the same as for research reports and patents and higher than other forms.

CONTROL OF PERIODICALS
There are many bibliographies and lists of periodicals issued for various papers and for various audiences which can be used to trace the existence of and to ascertain details of publisher, price etc.

Computer periodicals: The most comprehensive listing of computer periodicals so far published is the *World list of computer periodicals* (NCC, 1971). This is an alphabetic listing of well over 700 periodicals and other regularly produced serials (such as loose leaf data books and annual reviews). It is also a union catalog (see chapter 26). Unfortunately it is much less useful than it might have been, since it does not include any information about publishers or have any useful indexes, *eg* to countries or subjects. It is, however, particularly good in chronicling the various changes of name, amalgamations, translations etc that have occurred. A second edition will be published in 1973 that will incorporate the missing features.

In the meantime however we must turn elsewhere for fuller information, and the best lists of computer periodicals are those to be found as the lists of periodicals scanned by the individual abstracting services. An older list which is still of some use is the ' Classified directory of information processing periodicals ' in *Information processing journal* 1(1) 1962, 3-17. *Computer & information systems* publishes in each issue a source directory and a publisher directory.

Other abstracting journals which publish full information are *Computer abstracts* (in the annual index), *Computing reviews* (occasionally), *Data processing digest* (each issue) and *Computer and control abstracts*. The latter publishes a complete list of periodicals abstracted by the INSPEC Services in its index issues. Supplementary lists appear in the monthly issues

—usually every month. *New literature on automation* lists in each issue the titles of the periodicals abstracted, but includes only the town of publication rather than full details.

The other important source is the section on automation in *Ulrich's international periodicals directory* (14th edition 1971). This has international coverage of about 46,000 periodicals and includes computers and data processing, in addition to operational research and documentation.

General lists of periodicals: Particularly for periodicals which are not covered by the abstracting services, in order to check details, it may be necessary to go to one of the national lists of periodicals produced by either the book trade or as a reference publication by the national library. The book trade directories generally provide very good coverage of commercial and society periodicals, but cover less well newsletter and publications from other organisations. The main British list is *Willing's press guide* which has appeared annually since 1871 and has a subject index. In the United States some 20,000 periodicals appear in *Ayers directory: newspapers and periodicals* (annual), and in the *Standard periodical directory* (3rd edition 1969), which is arranged by subject groups with an alphabetical index.

Subject classified lists appear for German scientific journals (*Verzeichnis der deutschen wissenschaftlichen zeitschriften*), and for Russian periodicals (*Letopis' periodicheskikh izadii SSSR*). Similar alphabetical or classified lists exist for other countries.

House journals are rarely covered to any degree of completeness, and specialist lists usually exist for this type of periodical. British ones appear in *British house journals* (British Association of Industrial Editors). This is arranged alphabetically by firm, but does give information on the trade of the firm and whether the journal is intended for internal or external consumption. American house journals are listed in the *Printers Ink directory of house organs* (annual).

New periodicals: The appearance of new British periodicals is noted under the appropriate class numbers (and under the heading 'Periodicals' in the index) in the *British national bibliography*. International coverage of new periodicals is given by two major works. The US Library of Congress publishes *New serial titles* (monthly 1953-), which is an alphabetical list cumulating annually and quinquennially. A useful companion publication is *New serial titles—classed subject arrangement,* which lists periodicals by Dewey decimal classification class numbers. It appears monthly but does not, unfortunately, cumulate. *New periodical titles* (Butterworths, 1964-) appears quarterly and updates BUCOP and the *World list of scientific periodicals* (see chapter 26). It cumulates annually into a comprehensive list and a list of scientific periodicals only. A quinquennial cumulation also appears. Indexes of sponsoring bodies and of library symbols are included and the publication is, in fact, computer produced. Both *New serial titles* and *New periodical titles* are more than just periodicals lists as they also include libraries holdings (see chapter 26).

4 ACADEMIC PERIODICALS

THE NEXT THREE chapters describe individual periodicals arranged by countries (US, UK, European and other countries), and alphabetically within each country. Not all periodicals have comments attached, especially where their scope is clear from the title, and the lists are not comprehensive, but the periodicals included are the major ones in each country. Comprehensive lists and more bibliographical details can be found in the *World list of computer periodicals* (a second edition of which is due to be published in early 1973).

UNITED STATES

AEDS journal (1967-) contains lengthy research level papers on the applications of computers to education.

Communications of the ACM (1958-) reports original work at the working programmer level. The papers cover most areas of computing, and there are sections devoted to letters, ACM news, general news, coming events and a calendar. All new and proposed ANSI standards are published. There is a regular algorithms column which publishes algorithms in Algol, Fortran or PL/1. These are republished in *Collected algorithms from CACM*.

Computers and biomedical research (1967-).

Cybernetics (1965-) is the US translation of the USSR research journal *Kibernetika*.

Engineering cybernetics (1963-) is a translation of *Tekhnicheskaya kibernetika,* and is sponsored by IEEE. It is probably the most important Soviet journal in the areas of general systems design (including computers) and control theory.

IEEE translations on automatic control (1956-).

IEEE translations on computers (1952-) consists of research papers and short communications. The range of interests of this journal is wide, but does tend to exclude numerical analysis and software—concentrating upon hardware, logic and switching circuits and theory, etc. There is a large review section with long signed reviews. There is a good annual index to the journal. An important section of the journal is the 'Abstracts of computer literature', which gives good abstracts of a selected range of journals and report literature, mainly in the areas of interest of the *Transactions*. A fuller description appears in chapter 14.

IEEE transactions on systems, man and cybernetics (1960-) publishes research papers in this general area and covers a very wide range of 'systems'.

Information and control (1957-) deals with the more theoretical aspects of logic and switching theory, communication theory, automata and formal languages.

Information sciences (1968-) publishes research papers in a very wide area, *eg* artificial intelligence, metatheory, logic, formal languages, etc.

International journal of computer and information sciences (1971-) publishes research papers in virtually all aspects of computing except hardware design; in particular, areas such as software engineering, MIS, data structures are emphasised.

Journal of the ACM (1954-) reports original research, especially in the areas of metatheory and numerical analysis. All papers are aimed at the research scientist. There is a KWIC cumulative index for 1954-1963. Each paper has keywords and CR categories attached.

Journal of computational physics (1966-) contains a large amount of material on the treatment of mathematical equations, as it deals with data handling and the mathematical description of physical processes.

Journal of computer and system sciences (1967-) covers the formal and theoretical aspects of computers, *eg* formal aspects of programming, formal languages, logic and switching theory, automata, etc.

Journal of cybernetics (1971-) is the official journal of the American Society of Cybernetics, and publishes lengthy highly technical research papers in automata, game and information theories, artificial intelligence as well as cybernetics. An interesting feature is a translation supplement in which major papers from other countries (primarily USSR and Japan) are abstracted.

Journal of library automation (1968-).

Mathematical systems theory (1967-).

Mathematics of computation (1943-) is published by the American Mathematical Society, and is ' a journal devoted to advances in numerical analysis, the application of computational methods, mathematical tables, high speed calculators and other aids to computation '. In addition to the numerical analysis papers, there are reviews of mathematical tables and of books. A microfiche is included with each issue.

Pattern recognition (1969-) is the journal of the Pattern Recognition Society, and publishes research contributions in this area.

Rutgers journal of computers and the law (1970-) is a scholarly journal covering the two interactions of computers and law, *ie* applications to legal work and administration, and the legal implications of computer use (theft, evidence, software protection, etc).

SIAM journal on control (1963-).

SIAM journal on numerical analysis (1964-).

' SIC ' and ' SIC ' periodicals: These are the publications of the Special Interest Groups and Committees of the ACM. There are about 20 of them and they are all of considerable interest. Some reach a high academic standard, *eg SIGPLAN notices,* and often publish conference papers. Many of them regularly publish bibliographies, and they all contain news. They are regularly listed in the *Communications of the* ACM and it is unfortunate that they are not better known in the UK.

Simulation (1964-) covers analog, digital and hybrid simulation. It is very attractively produced and carries some society news as well as the excellent technical articles.

Soviet automatic control (1967-) is a translation of *Avto-*

32

matyka, the journal of the Ukrainian Institute of Cybernetics. Again this is a highly technical journal in the areas of control, pattern recognition, simulation, bionics, etc.

Systems computers controls (1970-) contains translations of computer papers originally published in the *Transactions of the Institute of Electronics and Communications Engineers of Japan,* and occasionally in other Japanese journals. It covers systems theory, computer design, automatic control and aspects of software and programming.

UNITED KINGDOM

Algol bulletin (1959-) is the most theoretical of all the individual language bulletins, and the recent work on Algol 68 has produced many interesting papers for the Algol specialist, on programming techniques and, *eg,* data structures.

Automatica (1963-) is published by Pergamon Press for the International Federation of Automatic Control, and, whilst not strictly concerned with computers, has many papers describing and analysing applications.

Computer journal (1958-) is the research journal of the British Computer Society. It publishes about 20 papers on all aspects of computing (although there is considerable emphasis on numerical analysis). There is a regular algorithms column and book reviews.

Computers in biology and medicine (1970-).

Information storage and retrieval (1963-) is primarily concerned with computer applications in this area.

International journal of biomedical computing (1970-) publishes research papers on the applications of all types of computers to medicine and the biosciences generally.

International journal of computer mathematics (1964-) has had a somewhat chequered career. By 1971, only 2 volumes had been published. With volume 3, the journal will appear in two parts: Programming languages: theory and methods; and Computational methods. Both will be theoretically orientated, although the latter section will be user-orientated.

International journal of control (1963-) is mainly concerned

33

with the theoretical aspects of machines and process control and automation.

International journal of man-machine studies (1969-) is another journal in a field which includes such areas as pattern recognition, learning, systems theory, cybernetics and bionics.

International journal for numerical methods in engineering (1969-) seems to publish mostly material on structural engineering, and is aimed at promoting a cross-fertilisation between structural engineering, heat transfer, fluid mechanics, network theory and optimal system design.

International journal of systems science (1970-) publishes research papers on the theory and practice of mathematical models, simulation, optimisation and control with especial reference to large scale systems.

Journal of computers and structures (1971-) is a research journal in the area of structural engineering.

Journal of statistical computation and simulation publishes research papers in areas of statistics which are related to or dependent upon the computer.

Journal of systems engineering (1969-) publishes research contributions on this topic considered as a general concept, and on the systems approach applied in particular areas, such as industrial plant, economic systems information systems, etc. It should be of increasing value to computer professionals.

Kybernetes is a new journal on ' the inter-disciplinary science of cybernetics in its widest sense ', *eg* artificial cybernetics, ecosystems, bio- and neuro-cybernetics, simulation, etc.

Software practice and experience (1969-) covers software in the strict sense of the word at a fairly high level.

EUROPE

German language

Acta informatica (1971-) is one of some half a dozen journals which have appeared in recent years covering the general areas of information systems, software engineering, systems programming, data management, automata theory and formal

34

languages, interactive and graphic computing, etc in one journal. It is published by Springer-Verlag, Germany.

Angewandte informatik (*Applied informatics*) (1959-) is a journal at about the same level as *Computer journal*. It mainly deals with mathematical material, although there are a substantial number of papers on programming, etc. Its previous title was *Elektronische datenverarbeitung*.

Beitrage zur linguistik und informationsverarbeitung (1963-) publishes research contributions on the applications of computers to linguistics.

Computing: archives for electronic computing (1966-) is an Austrian quarterly which publishes in German and English, original papers and review articles in electronic computer methods and applications. It excludes data processing and computer technology and has a strong numerical analysis bias. There are book reviews.

Elektronische informationsverarbeitung und kybernetik (1965-) publishes East European contributions in metatheory, automata, bionics, etc.

Kybernetik (1960-) West Germany.

Numerische mathematik (1959-) is a West German journal which specialises in numerical analysis, publishing papers in both English and German. A special issue of this journal was devoted to the Algol 68 report.

Regelungstechnik und prozessverarbeitung (1953-).

Holland

Artificial intelligence (1970-) is a very interesting research journal covering a wide range of fields in this general area.

Computer methods in applied mechanics and engineering (1972-) North Holland, Amsterdam.

Computer physics communications (1969-) is devoted to ' information on successful computed programs in physics '. Most ' papers ' are write-ups of programs preceded by a program abstract. A library of programs is maintained at Queen's University, Belfast.

Computer programs in biomedicine (1970-) publishes papers

on computer programs. The University of Uppsala maintains an index of these and other programs.

Computer studies in the humanities and verbal behaviour (1968-) contains research papers mainly in the areas of language and literature, with some articles on other subjects such as politics, art, archaeology and music, etc.

IAG *journal* (1968-) contains papers on administrative data processing. The subjects covered include education, software and programming techniques. As from 1972 this journal is called *Management informatics*.

Information processing letters (1970-) is the first ' letters ' journal in computing. It publishes short contributions very rapidly in the general fields of software, system architecture, applications and metatheory. No abstracts are published with the article, but keywords are included.

France and Belgium

Automatisme (1956-) deals with computer applications to industrial and scientific control problems.

Cybernetica (1958-) covers research in the areas of cybernetics, artificial intelligence, learning systems, etc, both in their technical and social aspects.

Proceedings of the International Association for Analog Computation (1958-) is a Belgian quarterly, publishing articles on analog and hybrid computation in English, French and German. It has a large abstracts section (although not so formally organised as a normal abstracting journal), which includes some 700-800 abstracts of research reports, theses, journal papers and conferences. Another section, ' Documents Reçus ' gives, arranged by journal, the contents lists of many journals and also covers books and conference proceedings. An extensive section notes forthcoming meetings, listing them by country.

Revue française d'informatique et de recherche operationelle (1958-) is the leading French academic journal, published in 3 series (each 3 times a year). The series are distinguished by the colour of their covers : blue contains material on computers, red on theory and methodology (statistics and mathematics) and green on operational research.

USSR

Avtomatika i telemekhanika (1934-) is one of the leading Russian journals publishing highly theoretical papers in a wide variety of computer topics—especially in metatheory, pattern recognition, artificial intelligence, bionics, logic and switching theory. It is translated as *Automation and remote control.*

Automatyka (1957-) is another highly theoretical Russian journal.

Kibernetika (1965-) is a Russian journal which publishes theoretical papers.

Tekhnicheskaya kibernetika (1963-) covers computer applications at a theoretical level, as well as areas such as pattern recognition, etc.

Zhurnal vychislitel'noi matematiki i matematicheskoi fiziki (1961-) is a Russian journal which publishes material on numerical analysis and the mathematics of physics. It is translated on a cover-to-cover basis as *USSR computational mathematics and mathematical physics.*

Other USSR periodicals can be found in the chapter on translations, where a complete list of translated periodicals is given.

Other European

Acta polytechnica scandinavica mathematics and computing machinery (1956-) publishes lengthy single papers with a very high mathematical content, usually on some aspect of applied mathematics or computing.

Algorytmy (1962-) Poland.

Archiwum automatyki i telemechananiki (1956-) Poland.

Automatika (1960-) is a Jugoslavian journal which publishes material in English.

BIT (1961-) publishes from Denmark research level contributions, with an emphasis on numerical analysis and algorithms, although there is often some material on programming. Most of the papers are in English.

Calcolo (1964-) an Italian quarterly publishes, in English and Italian, material on design, programming, logic and mathematics.

Economic computation and economic cybernetics (1966-). This is a particularly interesting Rumanian journal, with all the articles in English, for it is the only one specialising in economics and planning applications.

Informatyka (1965-), previously called *Maszyny matematyczne,* is one of the leading Polish journals and publishes very high quality papers.

Kybernetika (1965-) Czechoslovakia.

OTHER COUNTRIES

Infor Canadian journal of operational research and information processing (1971-) is a joint research publication of the Canadian Operational Research and Information Processing Societies, replacing *CORS journal.*

Information processing in Japan (1961-) is an annual translation of selected papers appearing in the previous year's *Joho shori* (1960-) (the journal of the Information Processing Society of Japan). Papers are technical ones on all aspects of computing, with particular emphasis on software.

Report of the Computer Centre, University of Tokyo (1968-) reports research, primarily in applications to the natural sciences.

5 COMMERCIAL PERIODICALS

AEDS monitor (1962-) is a monthly journal containing society news and more general articles on the applications of computers to education.

Business automation (1959-) is very much oriented to the overall concept of business systems and as well as computers covers microforms particularly. There is an annual directory issue (see chapter 20). There are regular new product sections, including one on software.

Computer (1966-) is the more newsy journal of the IEEE Computer Group. Although not neglecting software, its bias is towards hardware and systems design. It contains much information on group and other meetings, and other regular features include CAD newsletter, calls for papers, and the ' Repository ', which consists of papers available for evaluation either on hardcopy or microfilm. Up to March-April 1971 there was published a guide to current computer literature (author index, bibliography and KWIC index). The information, although no longer published, is now available through the Repository. The papers published are not as technical as those in *Transactions,* but are of good quality and are often review papers.

Computer decisions (1969-) concentrates on management applications, especially MIS.

Computer design (1962-), ' the magazine of digital electronics ', covers hardware design in practical engineering terms. There is an annual index to articles and each issue has a subject index to new product information.

Computer operations (1967-).

Computer services

Computers and automation (1951-) is the oldest commercial

periodical, which, over the past few years, has become concerned to a large extent with social issues. Technical computer articles appear with less frequency these days, but the news section, the monthly computer census, and new installations and contracts sections are still published. The June issue each year is also still published as *Computer directory and buyers guide,* and is described more fully in chapter 20.

Computers and the humanities (1966-) publishes articles on all aspects of the humanities, *eg* language and literature, music, art, archaeology, museums, etc as well as news, an annual bibliography and surveys of research projects, materials in machine readable form and programs.

Computing surveys (1969-) publishes formal survey and tutorial articles on all aspects of computing. The articles reach a very high standard and are especially valuable for obtaining an overview of a topic, *eg* microprogramming or picture processing. It is published by the ACM.

Data and communications design (1971-) is concerned with the whole computer/communications complex, and especially with economic factors, as well as technical, in view of the US trend away from a virtual monopoly situation in the communications industry.

Data dynamics (1971-) is a quarterly replacing *Data processing magazine.* It is very similar to its parent, and to such journals as *Datamation,* with a mixture of general and fairly technical articles for the working programmer.

Data management (1963-) is the official journal of the US Data Processing Management Association. There are general and DPMA news sections. The major articles (about 10-15 per issue) reach a very good standard at a not-too-technical level.

Datamation (1955-) has the largest circulation of all the US commercial journals. There are particularly good and extensive news and new product sections. For a time in 1971 this journal was published twice a month, which made it a lot easier to use, but it has now reverted to monthly publication.

EDP analyzer (1963-) is unusual in being a ' single-article ' journal. Each monthly issue consists only of one (excellent) article on some aspect of business data processing, *eg* data bases, computer personnel, etc.

Government data systems (1971-).

Information display (1964-) is the official publication of the Society for Information Display. It publishes technical articles for display engineers and users, together with new product and news sections.

Journal of data education

Journal of educational data processing (1964-).

Journal of systems management (1950-) is the publication of the Association for Systems Management. It concentrates upon business applications, DP management, etc.

Law and computer technology (1968-) is a magazine on all aspects of the relationship between law and the computer, *eg* applications to legal IR and administration, and increasingly on the computer industry problems of theft, security and software protection.

Modern data (1968-).

Software age (1967-).

UNITED KINGDOM

Computer aided design (1968-) publishes technical articles on CAD, extensive news and new product sections (including programs), and a few abstracts of technical literature.

Computer bulletin (1957-) is the news magazine of the British Computer Society. A few articles of general interest are published, but most of the bulletin is taken up by branch and national BCS news and new product news. A supplement includes late news and job advertisements. Book reviews are regularly published.

Computer education (1969-) publishes articles and news on computer education in schools. It includes reports on projects, as well as on teaching methods and techniques.

Computer management (1966-) is aimed largely at line managers, and consists very much of reworked press release material on recent products and services, as well as articles on topics of current interest.

Data management (1969-) is aimed at line managers, and consists of a few general articles and plenty of new product and service information.

Data processing (1959-) is aimed at middle and top management with fairly long articles on computer applications and equipment. Each issue usually has a supplement collecting a number of articles on a particular topic, *eg* bureaux, OCR, etc.

Data processing practitioner (1968-) is the journal of the Institute of Data Processing, and is mostly concerned with business applications of computing, especially in finance and accounting.

Data systems (1958-) is one of the main UK journals, offering a mixture of articles and news. The articles are aimed primarily at managers and computer personnel working in a business environment.

DPMA news is published by the Data Processing Managers Association, and includes articles as well as news. It could be a very good journal if its layout and appearance were improved.

Journal of the Institution of Computer Science (1970-) publishes articles on all aspects of computers. The first two volumes have shown a bias towards papers on human-computer interaction, with some general papers on programming and software developments.

Program (1966-) covers computer applications in libraries.

Software world (1969-) has a number of serious articles at a management/engineering level, on software and applications programs. The major portion of the journal consists of abstracts and news of programs. Also included are abstracts of reports and papers on software and programs.

EUROPE
German language

ADL nachrichten (1955-) is a society journal, and the scope tends towards the applications of computers in management and production control.

42

Archaographie: *archaologie und elektronische datenverarbeitung.*

Automatik (1955-) is of interest in the process and production control (including numerical control) fields.

Bürotechnik und automation (1960-) is the main West German periodical, covering office and business automation with good articles and much new product and services information.

Computer praxis (1968-) is published as a supplement to *Elektronische rechenanlagen.* It contains good engineering level articles and news.

Datenverarbeitung in steuer, wirtschaft und recht (1971-) covers computer applications in public administration and law.

Diagramm (1969-).

EDV in medizin und biologie (1970-).

Elektronische rechenanlagen (1959-) has particularly interesting articles on all aspects of computing, and in addition issues extremely good book-length supplements on computers and related topics, such as operational research.

Neue technik im büro (1956-), subtitled *Journal of data processing and office machines,* is an English language journal published by the East German firm of Zentronik. It reports in some detail on applications (mainly commercial) of East German computers, accounting machines, etc. Editions are also published in French and German.

Rechentechnik datenverarbeitung (1964-).

Zeitschrift für datenverarbeitung (1963-) publishes articles on commercial applications, and also includes new product information and a considerable amount of material on the computer industry.

Zeitschrift für organisation has well over half of its articles covering business applications. Much of the remainder covers closely related areas, such as OR and PERT / CPM, etc.

Holland

Informatie (1959-) is the main Dutch computer monthly, with good, commercially-orientated articles, book reviews, job and other advertisements and notes of new products.

43

Informatie nederlandse lexicologie (1970-) is approximately the Dutch equivalent of *Computers and the humanities.*

France

Bulletin de l'Iria (1969-) contains information on the work carried out at this French research establishment.

L'Informatique (1970-) is intended primarily for management.

Informatique et gestion (1958-) has long articles of good quality.

TA informations (1960-) covers various areas of the applications of computers to language, including IR, machine translation, linguistics, etc.

Zero un informatique—management (1967-) is one of the major French monthlies, with good quality articles aimed at the working computer professional, in a commercial environment primarily. The annual census of computer installations in France is summarised in the June issue.

Other European

Automatic data processing information bulletin (1967-) is published by the International Social Security Association, and contains articles on central and local government applications.

Automatizace (1958-) covers industrial process and production control applications mainly. There is a regular column on the characteristics of digital computers, looking at one machine (or range) each issue.

Automazione e automatismi (1957-) includes much material on computers especially applied to process control.

Clave is a Spanish journal, which has some articles together with a great deal of new product information.

Data behandling (1961-) is a well produced commercial journal with emphasis on business systems and programming. There is a considerable amount of new product information.

Information review, La revista dell'informazione (1970-) is an Italian periodical which covers the ' politics, economics, management, science, technology and sociology of informa-

44

tion '. Each issue contains the same articles in Italian and in English.

Inorga is a Czech journal, which mainly covers computer applications to the control of industrial processes and to production management.

Mechanizace automatizace administrativy (1961-) is a Czech journal covering business applications.

Moderne databehandling Norway.

Sistemi i automazione (1955-) is an Italian journal covering business applications.

Vyber (1968-) is a Czech journal with a mixture of news and a substantial number of good articles on commercial applications and programming.

OTHER COUNTRIES

Australian computer journal (1967-) seems to be primarily concerned with commercial applications and programming techniques, with articles aimed at the working analyst or programmer.

Canadian datasystems (1969-) follows very much the pattern of a normal commercial journal—concentrating upon Canadian matters, of course. The December issue each year includes a directory listing firms, products and equipment charts.

Canadian Information Processing Society magazine (1970-), as well as society news and articles, publishes as separate issues annual surveys of installations and of salaries.

Data trend (1964-) is an Australian monthly offering articles and a lot of news about the Australian and New Zealand computer scene.

ICA—information (1969-) is published in Israel for the Intergovernmental Council for ADP, and consists of articles and reports on the use of computers in government.

JIPDEC report (1970-) is especially valuable for its reports (with many statistics) on various aspects of the Japanese computer industry, as well as on JIPDEC activities.

South African computer bulletin (1958-) is the publication of the Computer Society of South Africa. As from 1972 it has merged with the magazine *Systems* to become *Systems—the journal of the Computer Society of South Africa.* Articles are published in English and Afrikaans.

Victorian computer bulletin is published by the Victoria Branch of the Australian Computer Society. It contains some news with, usually, one substantial article.

6 NEWS AND SPECIAL PERIODICALS

ADP newsletter (1956-), published fortnightly by the Diebold organisation, consists of a four page introductory and survey article on some aspect of computers and their applications to business. During the year surveys of the field and censuses of the US and European markets are published.

Arithmoi is one of the many newsletters in the humanities area which have begun to be published in the last few years.

Calculi (1967-) is a bi-monthly newsletter issued by the Department of Classics at Dartmouth College (US). It reports on computer applications to classical literature and includes a bibliography of recent papers, reports, etc.

CIS newsletter (1964-) covers recent developments in computer typesetting.

Computer age (1971-) is one of a series of news journals from EDP News Services Inc of Washington DC. This one covers the international computer industry, and consists of in-depth analyses and brief items. Other journals from this publisher are *EDP daily, EDP weekly, Peripherals weekly* and *Software digest* (see below).

Computer daily (1969-) contains short news items on all aspects of the computer industry.

Computer digest (1966-) is a monthly general newsletter covering business applications and new software, etc.

Computer and medieval data processing bulletin (1971-) is one of a crop of humanities-orientated journals and newsletters. This one is published by the Medieval Academy of America, and is concerned with the application of computers to medieval studies.

47

Computer newsfront (1969-) is a weekly news magazine on computers, data processing and data communications. It seems to be good on company financial information and there is an index.

Computerworld (1967-) is a very thick newspaper-format journal reporting on mainly US news. There are separate sections covering software, hardware and company and financial information.

Computing newsletter for schools of business (1968-) contains news items on computer education and educational applications in schools and colleges. There are regular book reviews and notes on programs—especially business games. Approximately annually there is a large bibliography of books.

Computing newsline (1964-).

Data automation digest (1963-).

Data processing for education (1962-) covers educational applications and computer applications news items.

Digital computer newsletter (1948-) is the oldest existing computer periodical (excluding periodicals which turned into computer ones), and is published by the Office of Naval Research. It has sometimes been published on its own and sometimes as part of the *Journal of the ACM* (1954-1957), and the *Communications of the ACM* (1958-1960).

D P focus (1968-) seems to specialise in company information.

EDP daily (1969-) consists of short news items about the US industry. There is a monthly index.

EDP industry report (1964-). This journal provides vital economic statistics, accurate analysis and predictions for the market researcher and those interested in the computer industry.

EDP weekly (1960-) complements *EDP daily* by longer in-depth analysis of the US industry.

Fastline monthly (1963-).

Finite string (1964-) is the monthly newsletter of the Association for Computational Linguistics. Of particular interest is the regular bibliographic section.

Graphic communications weekly (1968-).

Information retrieval and library automation (1965-).

Information week (1966-) is a newspaper format journal reporting US news.

Micrographics news and views (1970-) is one of a considerable number of journals at the interfaces between computers, publishing and microforms.

Micrographic weekly (1970-).

Peripherals weekly (1968-) includes company product and personnel news, as well as information on contracts awarded and government procurements.

Simulation in the service of society (1971-) is an interesting news magazine, which has grown out of discussions in *Simulation* on the feasibility of a ' world simulation '. This magazine is one of the visible signs of computer professionals' awareness of the social power of computers.

Software digest (1968-) is very similar in content to *Peripherals weekly,* but concentrates on software and applications programs. It includes two new literature sections—one on books and reports and the other on journal articles.

Systemation letter (1958-).

Time-sharing today (1970-) contains news and special reports on the US time-sharing industry.

UNITED KINGDOM

Bulletin of computer aided architectural design (1969-) is a duplicated news periodical covering literature, programs, forthcoming meetings. There are occasional articles.

Computer commentary is a monthly ' comment ', rather than news magazine, written by Richard H Williams in a distinctive personal style.

Computer news (1960-) is published as a supplement to *Computer abstracts* and includes about 8 pages of UK news.

Computer weekly (1966-) is the main UK news periodical, with good coverage of domestic and foreign news as well as one main article, many pages of job advertisements, and lengthy editorial comment.

Computer weekly international (1969-) is a monthly supplement to *Computer weekly* concentrating upon foreign (especially European) news and feature articles. There are many job advertisements as well.

Dataweek (1966-) is a weekly newspaper with plenty of job advertisements. One page usually presents a featured company.

EDP Europa report (1969-). For the person interested in marketing or the computer industry, this journal, and its sister US publication, is the most important that can be read. The analyses are based upon accurate statistics, and predictions seem to be good. There is a wealth of economic statistics published.

Geocom bulletin (1968-) is a monthly news periodical devoted to the applications of computers to the earth sciences.

Microinfo (1970-) covers the general area of microfilm and computers.

Page (1969-) is the bulletin of the Computer Arts Society, and as well as articles and notes on this topic seems to include items on the sociological impact of computers, and the social responsibilities of the computer profession.

Peripherals bulletin (1971-) is published twice monthly, and includes news and analysis on equipment designed to collect, transmit and convert data.

Software monthly (1970-) updates *Software world* with news of companies and programs.

Time sharing news (1968-) carries general comment on the time sharing industry in the US and UK, with news on companies, hardware and programs.

EUROPE
German language

Büro-markt-pressdienst is an Austrian newsletter in the general office field which includes a lot of computer items.

Die computer zeitung (1970-) is a newspaper format periodical reporting computer news, jobs, etc.

Datascope (1970-) is another German news journal.

50

Holland

Computable (1968-) is a Dutch monthly in newspaper size with mostly news items and new product information.

IAG communications (1967-). This journal reports on activities of IAG member countries. It frequently gives economic statistics of countries or of particular sectors.

France

Electroniques actualités has, as does *Electronics weekly* in the UK, a good coverage of new computer equipment and general computer news.

Informatique selecto (1970-).

Zero un informatique—hebdo (1967-) is the main French news periodical, with short reports on current news and job advertisements.

Other European

Modern datateknik (1965-) is a Swedish fortnightly news magazine in newspaper size. There are one or two major articles with plenty of advertisements and new product information.

OTHER COUNTRIES

ILTAM newsletter (1969-) reports on the computer industry in Israel, and frequently includes economic statistics.

SPECIAL PERIODICALS

There are a number of what can only be described as ' special ' periodicals. They are neither academic, commercial nor news. In general they are described more fully elsewhere :

Computer characteristics review consists only of equipment characteristics and is more fully described in chapter 21. *Computer characteristics digest* is similar and is described in the same chapter.

Computer survey (1962-) is unusual in being primarily a record of computer installations in the UK, published in periodical form. It occasionally has articles and news, notes and new equipment. The statistical material follows a regular pattern throughout the year; March/April, new entries and significant changes, UK users, summary by user industry; May/June, export installations and orders; July/August, new entries and significant changes, UK users, summary by manufacturer and machine types, buyers guide to peripheral and associated equipment; September/October, export installations and orders, who's who and personnel survey; November/December, full alphabetical list of users, summary of applications; January/February, export installations and orders, survey of computer service bureaux.

Computer time review consists of abstracts describing computer installations with time to sell on their machines. A certain amount of directory information concerning company services is also included.

Computer equipment guide (1970-) is a journal consisting of tear-out reader service cards together with a directory section in the centre pages.

CC sellers (1971-) is a new service which gives the prices of computer systems and peripherals in two series—medium and small sized.

Informatique digest (1971-) is also a reader service card journal of somewhat more bulk than the UK ones. It is published by Editions Tests (Paris).

Time sharing system scorecard has details of research and commercial time sharing services including brief details of machine, languages, packages, etc.

Computerware exchange (1970-) contains only advertisements of services, jobs, programs, etc.

HOUSE JOURNALS

Most computer firms publish some form of journal of their own, which can range from a simple four page advertising sheet to a periodical publishing research that is qualitatively

52

the equal of any published in those journals described as academic.

UNITED STATES

(a) *Academic*: There are a few academic house journals published. *IBM journal of research and development* (1957-) is published monthly, and contains articles describing original work done in all areas of IBM research. There is a section of abstracts of technical papers by IBM authors in other journals, and a listing of new US patents issued to IBM. *IBM systems journal* (1962-) is published quarterly and contains material on programming, system architecture, time sharing, etc. Honeywell publish the research level *Honeywell computer journal* (1967-), which, in 1971, was made more openly available on a subscription basis. Finally, *Bell system technical journal* has a considerable amount of material on computers and their applications—especially to electronic circuits and to communications systems.

(b) *Commercial*: IBM publish many journals at this level. *IBM technical disclosures bulletin* (1958-) gives short technical descriptions of circuits and components somewhat similar to abbreviated patent disclosures; *IBM computing report in science and engineering* (1965-) reports on applications of IBM equipment in these areas, while *Data processor* (1956-) performs a similar function for the business world. Sperry Rand make a similar distinction (although the articles have considerably more depth than the two IBM ones just mentioned) with the *Sperry Rand engineering review* and *Univac input for modern management* (1964-). *Decuscope* (1962-) tends to concentrate upon business applications of DEC equipment (PDP computers). *Bonner & Moore summary* (1966-) has a 2-3 page article on a fairly general topic. *The Leasco magazine* (1970-) is well produced and carries good general articles. *Burroughs clearing house* (1916-) is another at this level, as is *Hewlett-Packard journal* (1949-).

(c) *News*: These are the most prolific of all magazines. All manufacturers and service companies produce newsletters in one form or another, and obviously space cannot be given to describe all of them. The following are a representative sample: *Computer talk* (3M Company, 1967-), *Calcomp newsletter, Campus computing newsletter* (IBM), *SDS interface, Burroughs data.*

(a) *Academic*: There are no UK periodicals at this level.

(b) *Commercial*: There are not very many of these either. Honeywell publish *Computer age* (1965-), which is a mixture of news and articles about applications of Honeywell equipment. *Computers and management* (NCR, 1967-) is somewhat similar. *Interface* (NCC, 1967-) contains news and articles based upon lectures given at NCC seminars and meetings. From a software house there is the *SPL review* (1969-), which has articles of general interest.

(c) *News*: These are the most prolific. ICL publish *ICL computer international* (1968-), which has superseded the more substantial *ICT data processing journal,* and *ICL update* (1970-). IBM have *Link* (1967-). There are also such other news journals as *Scicon Computer Bureau newsletter* (1970-), *Burroughs computer newsletter for management, Argus newsletter* (1968-), *Data logic bulletin* (1969-) and *Decnews* (Digital Equipment Ltd).

(a) Academic: The most significant periodical at this level is *Metra* from the Metra Consulting Group in Paris.

(b) *Commercial*: There are a lot of good commercial-level journals published in Europe and elsewhere, eg *ICL-data* (Sweden), *Revue CEGOS informatique* (CEGOS, France), *Die lochkarte* (Univac, 1935-), *Siemens data report* (1966-), *Hitac* (Hitachi, 1966-), *IBM nachrichten* (1931-), *Bull General Electric berichten* (1962-), and *Bull General Electric systèmes d'information review* (1968-).

(c) *News*: All major manufacturers publish news journals, *eg De computer* (Honeywell, Amsterdam, 1969-), *ICL computer nieuws* (Amsterdam, 1967-), *National-post* (NCR, Germany), *Mahashovot* (IBM, Israel), etc.

7 RESEARCH REPORTS AND GOVERNMENT PUBLICATIONS

THE TECHNOLOGICAL GROWTH caused by the two world wars, the polarisation of the world into two political blocs after the second world war, and the massive and increasing involvement of governments in the sponsorship of research, are factors which have all contributed to make research reports a very important source of information, yet one which is still often overlooked in the general search for information.

The term ' research report ' is commonly applied only to those reports which arise from government sponsored research or from government agencies, but it should not be forgotten that independent organisations such as universities, research associations and industrial firms also issue them.

The value of the research report lies in the fact it deals with advanced or specialised, pure and applied research, usually in much more detail than could be given in a journal paper. In addition, other types of material can be issued as research reports which it is difficult to imagine being published in any other way, such as translations, programming manuals and conferences. Broadly speaking, about 2,000-3,000 reports of interest to the computer are issued each year.

In spite of their value, there are certain aspects of research reports which can be traps for the unwary. Many are only progress reports, to be superseded by final ones, and they say little more than that work on a project was continued. Many, too, are later published in journals, or are read at conferences with more or less detail than appears in the original report, so that to be sure of finding all the information required, a great deal of redundant material must be read or scanned.

Among the major producers of reports are US government agencies and contractors, and much work is carried out in pure computer technology and science, as well as in applications to most fields of knowledge. The main agency in the USA which distributes research reports is the National Technical Information Service (NTIS) which changed its name from the Clearinghouse for Federal Scientific and Technical Information (CFSTI) in 1971. It distributes to the general public all unclassified reports generated by government agencies and contracts, and announces them through the abstracting journal later described. The change in name represents a greater emphasis on the distribution of commercial, non-scientific reports especially from such bodies as the Department of Commerce.

Reports are usually cited by author, title, originating organisation and report number. The latter is a code number usually consisting of letters and numbers which, for US reports distributed through NTIS, generally has the letters 'AD' or ' PB ' (although any one report may have other numbers as well). If a report which is sought has been cited by report number only, without any indication of the originator, it is possible to trace the latter by means of the *Dictionary of report series codes* (Special Libraries Association, 1962; second edition in preparation).

Government publications, while including many research reports, are generally taken to refer to those publications which originate from government departments and, in contrast to the majority of reports, are openly for sale, usually through a national agency such as HMSO or the US Government Printing Office.

Details of some sample reports appear below to illustrate the various types:

A Government research reports

1 Ballistic Research Labs, Aberdeen Proving Ground. *A library system for magnetic tapes,* by G B Thompson. January 1968. BRL-TN-1680 (AD 667364).

2 Foreign Technology Div, Wright-Patterson AFB. *Computer*

techniques by A M Oranskii. October 1967. FTD-HT-23-644-67 (AD 667646). This is a translation of a Russian book originally published in 1964.

3 Argonne National Laboratory. *Proceedings of a conference on the applications of computer methods to reactor problems.* May 1965. ANL-7050. This has no ' AD ' number, since it is a report issued through the Atomic Energy Commission.

B *Contract research for the government*

1 Wisconsin Univ Mathematics Research Center. *Machine language programming for the CDC 3600* by J M Yohe. August 1967. MRC-TSR-721 (AD 666188). This report was performed under contract from the US Army Research Office.

C *Non-contract research*

1 IBM. *Selective dissemination of new scientific information with the aid of electronic processing equipment* by H P Luhn. 1959.

2 California Univ, Berkeley. *Reference manual time sharing system* by L P Deutsch *et al.* November 1967. R-21 (AD 677634). D *Government publications.*

1 Department of Scientific and Industrial Research. *Automatic data processing* by D W Morley. HMSO, 1961.

2 National Physical Laboratory. *Modern computing methods.* HMSO, second edition 1961.

The major reports abstracting service, which is a model of good abstracting (though not, regrettably, of good subject indexing), is the semi-monthly *Government reports announcements* (GRA)—previously *US Government research and development reports* (USGRDR), which has been produced under various titles since 1946, and announces over 60,000 reports of US government sponsored research and development and translations each year. It includes all unclassified reports and translations released to the public by the Atomic Energy Commission (AEC), Department of Defense (DOD), National Aeronautics and Space Administration (NASA), and many other US government departments and agencies. It is computer produced from records produced by CFSTI, AEC, DOD and NASA.

GRA now includes all translations sponsored or produced by

governments (not only the US) since the demise of *Technical translations* (at the end of 1967), and also includes reports from a variety of other (mostly governmental) organisations, such as the National Research Council (Canada), NATO, the Royal Aircraft Establishment (Farnborough, UK) etc.

As previously mentioned, NTIS reports start with an AD or PB prefix, and these form the bulk of the entries. Other frequently encountered numbers have the prefixes 'JPRS', 'TT' (both translations), and 'N' (items taken from STAR). Other report prefixes such as NAA-SR, BNL, LA and very many others usually signify details taken from *Nuclear science abstracts* (NSA).

The format of GRA has changed a great deal over the years, but it now (1972) consists of two sections: research and development reports and translations (the main part); and a 'report locator' list (cross referencing the main report number to the subject section of the main part).

The reports are arranged by subject groups, and the main categories of interest are: 9B (computers), 9C (electronic and electrical engineering), 9D (information theory), 9E (subsystems), 5B documentation and information technology), 12A (mathematics and statistics) and 12B (operations research). The information given is: title, author affiliation, publisher (if different from affiliation), author(s), date, number of pages, report number(s), contract and/or grant number(s), subject descriptors, abstract, accession number and prices. In each section, as well as the abstracted reports, there are cross references to reports in other sections, but, with computers at least, this form of cross referencing is not very effective and the only way to trace all reports on computer applications is through a page by page search.

Indexes to GRA are now provided by the semimonthly *Government reports index* (GRI) (1966-) which is the latest (and one hopes the best and most permanent) in a long series of somewhat doubtful and erratic indexes to USGRDR. It provides author, organisation, contract/grant number, report/accession number and subject indexes to GRA, NSA and STAR. This index now cumulates quarterly and annually (1968-).

Other services from NTIS include an enquiry service, GRA on magnetic tape, GRI cumulated from 1964-69 on microfilm, Fast Announcements Service which highlights selected reports of commercial significance and is issued in 57 separate subject categories, Government Reports Topical Announcements, which announces all NTIS documents in 35 separate categories, and Selective Dissemination of Microfiche, whereby fiche are automatically distributed at approximately one-third of their normal price.

The other important source for research reports is *Scientific and technical aerospace reports* (STAR), which is the semi-monthly abstracting service issued by NASA. Although primarily containing material of interest to the aerospace field, there is a large amount of much more general material on computers. Some of this comes from basic research on computers sponsored by NASA and the US Air Force, some from reports first announced in GRA, and some from aerospace organisations who issue reports on computer theory and practice which have a more general application. STAR is particularly strong in reports from Eastern and Western Europe, and in nuclear energy reports. It is, in fact, from such organisations as EURATOM and the British Atomic Energy Research Establishment (AERE) that many of the more general reports come.

As well as being indexed in GRI, STAR has its own indexes which cumulate quarterly and annually. The subject indexing is of a much higher quality than that of GRI.

Another most useful source is NSA, which also includes many reports of a more general nature as well as reports applied to atomic energy.

Until the experimental production by the National Lending Library of the current awareness tool *British research and development reports* (monthly, 1966-), there was no single source for announcing British reports. This has also changed its name, to *NLL anouncement bulletin,* and includes reports, translations and theses available from NLL. It arranges material by subject groups but does not have any index. The other major service of NLL in this field is the supply of all NTIS, NASA and

USAEC documents on microfiche. A complete collection of all Rand Corporation documents is also held.

Other sources in Britain include the *British national bibliography,* accession lists of other libraries interested in this field, the lists put out by originators, *eg* computer manufacturers, and also users such as the UK Atomic Energy Authority (UKAEA).

The position in other countries varies considerably. Some make considerable efforts to include reports in their national bibliographies, while in others the equivalent of a national science library attempts to collect them and they appear in its accessions list.

Industrial research reports produced by individual companies are, for obvious reasons, usually secret. Those that are not, can be discovered and obtained in a number of ways : by personal contacts, by subscription to a mailing list, and by lists of their reports from those organisations which do list them, *eg* IBM, ICL and the Rand Corporation. IBM, via their ITIRC system, abstract their own manuals, reports and standards very well indeed in *IBM documents* (monthly).

Government publications other than reports are, on the whole, easy to discover and to obtain. Most countries have some form of catalog of their government publications, and, in addition, many of the more important titles in the computer field will appear in the current national bibliography, will be abstracted, and will also feature in journals as subjects of book reviews or literature notes. Three of the more important guides appear below.

Government publications (1897-) is published by HMSO and appears weekly, with monthly and annual cumulations. Arrangement is by issuing body with an author/subject index which is not entirely satisfactory. The index appears also in quinquennial cumulations.

Monthly catalog of United States government publications (US Government Printing Office, 1895-) lists some 25,000 items per year. The arrangement is by issuing body and there are monthly and annual subject and author indexes.

French publications are listed in the *Bibliographie de la France, supplément F : publications officielles* (1950-).

BIBLIOMETRIC CHARACTERISTICS

More than 5,200 research reports were published in 1966. These constituted 20.8% of the total literature. The most prolific countries publishing reports were the United States with 83.5% (40.4%), UK 5% (16%), and France, Israel and Western Germany with about 1.5% each. The number in brackets represents the percentage of that country's output which research reports constitute. It clearly shows the fact that in the United States, because of the structure of research and the good bibliographic control, the research report forms a major part of the literature unlike other countries such as the UK.

The most prolific sources for research reports are naturally enough GRA 50% and STAR 49%, with the computer abstracting services covering only 26% (CIS) and 15.5% (CA).

8 TRADE LITERATURE

THE TERM ' trade literature ' usually refers to the descriptive or publicity material issued by manufacturers or distributors in connection with the products they sell. It can at times refer also to house journals (see chapter 6), and to research reports (see chapter 7) produced by manufacturers. We shall restrict the term for the purposes of this chapter to advertising material, manuals and applications reports.

Trade literature apart from the purely factual hardware and software manuals, is a form of commercial advertising and therefore should be treated with a certain caution. Some trade literature, however, is produced in which the motive is the conveyance of knowledge rather than sales appeal, and even pure advertising sheets can be of considerable importance in giving details of new products, working specifications and technical data. In any case, advertising in the fields of technology is, on the whole, very different from general consumer advertising, with far less dependence on inflated claims, and more upon technical detail, so that the capabilities of the product are clearly explained to a sophisticated audience.

It goes without saying that all manufacturers produce some trade literature. What is perhaps unusual is that it is almost always well designed and produced, and a large amount of it is of considerable general interest for a specialist library and its clientèle.

We can divide trade literature into the following groups: firstly, one to four page advertising sheets, giving brief technical details and very little ' puffing '. Secondly, there are manuals produced by manufacturers for computers and peripherals— very often produced both as less technical introductory manuals, and with much more detail for experts. Typical of this type of material is the series of volumes known as the ' IBM systems reference library ', which covers hardware and software of all IBM machines and peripherals, the manuals for the ICL 1900 series, and so on. Standard software manuals are produced, since the implementation of the various languages differs for each machine.

Third is the specialist software for individual machines, *eg* the manuals for the Nineteen Hundred Indexing and Cataloging (NIC), for the Atlas Multiple Variate Counter, etc. Usually there are non technical introductory brochures for advertising the program, in addition to a full manual. Allied to this type of material are applications reports, which give information, in some cases very detailed, of successful applications of a manufacturer's machines or program package in particular situations.

Finally there is a miscellaneous class of trade literature which includes more general introductions to programming, to computers as a whole, and to specific computer languages. A point to be noted here is that many commercially published books started life as this type of literature, originally published internally within an organisation as material for training courses. (A clue to this may be whether the language discussed is solely one manufacturer's version, or whether any implementation is for the same manufacturer's machines.) Other material includes the ' General information manual ' and the ' Reference manual ' series from IBM (the latter has one of the clearest introductions to information retrieval yet published), and such works as ICL's *Techniques of computer management* (five loose-leaf volumes, 1966).

The bibliographic control of trade literature is difficult, since abstracting services rarely include this type of material, although a very good case can be made out for the inclusion of all material apart from straightforward advertising sheets, and possibly hardware reference manuals. Certainly, special program literature, applications reports and the more miscellaneous material should be abstracted, for this type of literature fulfils a definite and considerable need. *New literature on automation* is the only abstracting service which includes the latter categories at all, and the coverage is only confined to the material which enters the library of the Studiecentrum voor Informatica. An example is F Lambert *Considerations sur la programmation lineaire* (IBM European Education Center, 1960).

Most companies issue lists of their publications; IBM has a monthly abstracting bulletin with items mostly available to IBM personnel in microform, while others produce lists with more or less detail about the size of the publication, its date and amendments, etc. Apart from IBM, it is unusual to find any really comprehensive lists from a company. In general each division within a company produces its own.

Other sources of trade literature include the following: catalog services which provide trade literature in standard format in binders or in microform, *eg Electronic engineering index* and *Visual search microfilm file* (VSMF); the trade literature sections of commercial journals; trade exhibitions, such as the annual Business Efficiency Exhibition and the Radio and Electronic Components Show; finally, the mailing lists of manufacturers.

9 THESES

THESES ARE WRITTEN ACCOUNTS of original research work carried out by a candidate for a higher degree at a university or college. Since they consist of original research, those devoted to scientific subjects should be of interest to other scientists, and yet theses are one of the least known and least used sources of information. The main reason for this is that until fairly recently, when they have been available from a central clearinghouse, they have been available for purchase only, and not through the normal library interloan system. The only existing clearinghouse has been confined to US theses, and UK ones have been very difficult to obtain.

There is a large amount of research work being carried out, and the number of theses on computers and related topics is growing very fast. The only source for information about all UK theses is Aslib's annual *Index to theses*. It is an index only, without any abstracts, but does include details of the availability of theses from the holding universities. It is subject-arranged, with subject and author indexes. It is, unfortunately, considerably late in appearing.

An attempt has been made recently by the NLL to persuade all UK universities to lend doctoral theses to the NLL, where they will be microfilmed and made available on loan. This scheme, though admirable, is dependent upon the goodwill of the universities and upon listing in *NLL announcement bulletin*. Neither of these features are likely to make for a successful scheme since British universities have shown themselves in the past unwilling to give their theses wider currency. This is a surprising attitude, which contradicts all that universities—in other ways promoters of scientific and humanistic scholarship, with all that this implies in terms of free exchange of informa-

66

tion—represent. Additionally, whilst *NLL announcements bulletin* is a good current awareness tool, it is not indexed for retrospective searching.

US and Canadian theses are very well covered by *Dissertation abstracts* (monthly, 1938-), which is issued in two sections, one on the sciences and engineering, and one on the humanities and social sciences. There are good monthly and annual author and subject indexes. Long abstracts are given, and all theses reported are available on microfilm or as full-sized hard copy from the publishers. A computer-based search service is also available. NLL now receives a microfilm copy of all theses appearing in *Dissertation abstracts* (from 1970 onwards), which amounts to more than 25,000 a year. These are available on loan.

Abstracting journals have tended at various times to include theses (see also the next section for data on the 1966 situation). CCA uses *Dissertation abstracts* as one of its sources and includes the order number. CR includes theses from 1968 onwards and, in that year, attempted to include them retrospectively. The current coverage is about 25, but unfortunately they do not include any order information. CIS has, at various times, used *Dissertation abstracts* as a source, and for the periods that it did so is likely to be fairly comprehensive. Because of the considerable government funding of research at US universities, many theses appear in GRA and STAR, and these include material which does not appear in *Dissertation abstracts*.

All the major countries of computer interest list their theses in more or less helpful ways. France has the *Bibliographie de la France supplément D* (1882-), whilst the *Bulletin signalétique* has good coverage of French theses, and ones on computing will appear in Section 1. For Germany, there is the *Jahresverzeichnis der Deutschen hochschulschriften* (1885-), which allows a subject approach, and the journal *VDI zeitschrift* regularly includes lengthy abstracts and titles of German engineering theses.

A very useful survey of the general and specialist publications listing theses of fourteen countries, although naturally biased towards chemistry, is I R Stephens ' Searching for theses, dissertations and unpublished data ' in *Searching the chemical literature* pp 110-120 (American Chemical Society, 1961; Advances in Chemistry series no 30). A more general guide, reportedly listing 1,000 sources of information, is *Theses and dissertations* (Gale Research Co.).

BIBLIOMETRIC CHARACTERISTICS

A total of 347 theses was published in 1966, constituting 1·39% of the total literature. They were mainly published in the United States (81·5%) and the UK (11·5%). Oddly enough, these figures represent almost exactly the same percentage of each country's total output—2·6% and 2·4% respectively. Theses were badly covered by abstracting services then, with GRA being the most prolific source (although this was less than one-third) and STAR close behind. The computer abstracting journals CA and CR both covered only 11·8%; and those from CA came through GRA and were not consciously included. The situation has improved since then, with CCA including material from *Dissertation abstracts* and CR consciously expanding its coverage of theses.

10 PATENTS

A PATENT IS a monopoly for a period granted by the state to the owner of an invention to enable the invention to be exploited for the benefit of the owner and the community. It is a bargain between the community and the inventor for the benefit of both.

Patents are important because they cover recent advances in a particular technology, and may sometimes provide the only source of detailed descriptions of new processes, machinery, etc. In some cases the patent may even be the most detailed hardware and programming manual available.

A patent is granted for a period of sixteen years in the UK, and there are strict regulations concerning exactly what can be patented.

Patents are taken out in three stages: *a*) An application is made to the Patent Office and provisional protection given. The provisional specification does not give a detailed description, but is primarily for establishing a priority date. *b*) Within twelve months the complete specification must be filed. This gives a detailed description and lists the claims. When the complete specification is published, and up to twelve months after sealing, the patent is open to opposition on a number of possible grounds. *c*) Finally, acceptance is made (within about two years) and the patent sealed; at which time copies may be purchased. At each stage of the process the public is informed in the *Official journal* (*patents*).

The titles of patents are deliberately, in many cases, left vague to avoid informing competitors of the precise subject of the claim when notice of the application is made in the *Official journal* (*patents*). An example of this is British Patent 1015651, taken out by Sperry Rand Corporation and titled 'Processor'. In fact this is an electronic unit performing similar work to a computer, and intermediate, in cost and speed of operation, between tabulators and computers. This is a large patent (they may only run to two pages of text and one diagram), consisting of 128 pages of text and 183 sheets of diagrams containing 349 figures. Another very large patent is : IBM *Improvements in or relating to electronic data processing machines.* BP 1108800 3 April 1968 (1,319 pages + 495 sheets of drawings).

Most of the sources of information about patents are official publications of the Patent Office.

CURRENT INFORMATION ON PATENTS

1 *Searching by number*: The patent number is the item by which patents are usually cited in references etc, and is the key to the patent. Information about complete specifications is published weekly in the *Official journal* (*patents*). These are arranged by number, and represent the latest patents accepted. Information given includes the patentee, title and class numbers. Also arranged by patent number is the *Divisional allotment index to the abridgements of specifications,* which shows the division under which the new specification will appear in the abridgement volume. Each Wednesday the new patents are laid out in numerical order in the National Reference Library and many people search through them.

2 *Searching by name* (of the inventor and/or owner): A name index to the complete specifications appears each week in the *Official journal.*

3 *Searching by subject*: Under the classification divisions are listed the numbers of those patents falling within them, each week.

RETROSPECTIVE INFORMATION

1 *Searching by number*: The complete specifications are bound in numerical order, or, for very recent ones, in boxes in numerical order.

2 *Searching by name*: Name indexes (the *Index to names of applicants* . . .) are published in bound form for groups of 20,000 patents, with very brief titles and giving the complete

specification number. A card index (*Name index of latest acceptances*) to cover the gap between publication of the patent and of the printed index is maintained at the Patent Office in London.

3 *Searching by subject*: The *Abridgements of specifications* are published for groups of 20,000 patents. They consist of a brief general description and usually an illustration. They are in broad groups which cover one or more divisions of the classification; *eg*, there is one volume for G4-G6, which covers calculating, signalling, data handling (G4); education, advertising, music, recording (G5); nucleonics (G6). Within the volumes they are arranged numerically by patent number, which produces a very mixed order. In each volume there is a subject index, listing, under the detailed headings of each division of the classification, the numbers of the patents allotted to them, and a name index. To cover the time lag between publication of the patent and of the abridgement volume, one copy of the complete specification is filed under each division of the classification at the Patent Office. Abridgements are also filed in the same way as they will be published, *ie* in numerical order within groups.

To find the classification number for any subject, it is necessary to consult the *Reference index to the classification key* (1963) which consists, firstly of a catchword index, and then a classified sequence, by division and first heading (*eg*, G4 A), giving definitions and scope notes.

The *Classification key* itself is in classified order and is more detailed than the *Reference index*. Appropriate sections appear in each volume of abridgements.

The classification was changed in 1963 (from patent 940001 onwards), and there are thus two versions of the *Reference index* and the *Classification key*. To convert from the old to the new classification, and vice versa, there has been published, in one pamphlet, the *Classification key : forward concordance,* which leads from the old to the new numbers and the *Classification key : backward concordance,* which performs the opposite job.

To find the division number of a patent whose patent number is known, one can either look at the patent itself where the division number is printed at the head, or use the *Divisional allotment index to the abridgements of specifications*. This lists patents by number, giving their division, and is compiled for groups of 20,000 patents.

APPLICATIONS FOR PATENTS

The first notification that an application has been made appears in the *Official journal (patents)*, where applications are listed by name with the title and an application number, such as 23326/63.

Card indexes of applicants' names are maintained, in yearly sets, for the current and six preceding years. Under any one name arrangement is by date of application. The information given is title and application number.

Having an application number, it is possible through a series of ledgers with the entries arranged by application number to trace the subsequent history of the application—the complete specification number, or whether it was withdrawn or declared void.

There also appears in the *Official journal (patents)* an index by year and application number of the complete specifications published in that issue.

The above remarks apply, of course, only to British patents —analogous indexes appear for other countries such as USA, Germany etc. Some may be more helpful than the British indexes. For example, the *Official gazette of the United States Patent Office* contains illustrated abridgements in three classes —general and mechanical, chemical, electrical, and within these classes the patents are in numerical order (which seems to coincide with the classified order). Alphabetical and geographical indexes are provided.

The National Reference Library holds patents and patent gazettes from many countries (these are listed in their *Periodical publications . . .*).

Derwent Publications Ltd is a private British firm which

issues abstracts of specifications, both by country (*eg* Britain, Germany, France) and by subject, covering a number of countries (*eg Nuclear power patents bulletin*). Full details can be found in the *Derwent patents manual* (second edition 1964). Many consider that their abstracts are better than those of the Patent Office.

BIBLIOMETRIC CHARACTERISTICS
Patents contributed 10·85% of the published literature in 1966. This is a total figure of 2,716 items, and is a high percentage considering the general lack of interest shown in patents as an information source.

The main contributor countries to the patent literature are : USA 49·5% (12·5%), Japan 11·6% (40%), USSR 9·75% (9·2%), UK 7·8% (12·7%), France 5·9% (26·5%), West Germany 4·9% (12%), East Germany 4·8% (42·6%). Eleven other countries also produced computer patents. In each case the first percentage represents the country's contribution to the patent literature, whilst the second (in brackets), represents the contribution of patents to the total output of the country. It seems likely that the high second figure for Japan and probably France also is a consequence more of the poor coverage of other forms of literature rather than of the intrinsic importance of patents in these countries.

CONTROL OF PATENTS
Primary and complete control must always be through the national patent gazettes. If we consider the computer abstracting journals, we find that, in 1966, over 50% of the literature in RZA was patent literature from 18 countries—2,415 items. The next nearest was CA with 422 and RZK with 141.

For coverage of the major UK and US patents, however, it is sufficient to search CA and CCA, although this will by no means result in complete coverage, there being about 1,550 altogether from these two countries.

11 CONFERENCES

PROFESSIONAL MEETINGS are increasing rapidly in number and importance. They offer an opportunity for specialists to meet and discuss matters of common interest—stimulating each others' work. Verbal delivery of scientific papers at meetings may take the place of publication in a journal, and an investigation of conference papers showed that nearly half of those considered were not published elsewhere. The papers may also give the first indication of new work carried out by the speaker, and may be the only public report of that work for a long time. The project may be written up for a journal only when finally complete and the publication delay could be anything up to a year. Lastly, a common and important type of conference paper is that which reviews a field, or part of it, and forms a report on the ' state of the art '.

There are a large number of regular meetings in the computer field, as well as an even larger number of ' one-off' conferences on specific topics. The most important of the regular conferences are the Fall Joint Computer Conference (1962-; previously the Eastern Joint Computer Conference, 1951-1961), and the Spring Joint Computer Conference (1962-; previously the Western Joint Computer Conference, 1953-1961). Both of these are organised by the American Federation of Information Processing Societies and the proceedings are now published by AFIPS Press. In addition, a cumulative index to the proceedings from 1951-1970 has been published.

Other important and regular US conferences are the annual meeting of the Association for Computing Machinery (ACM), the proceedings of which have recently become freely available through a commercial publisher, and are abstracted by the major services; the semiannual meetings of the Data Processing Management Association, which are of a more general nature and are published as *Data processing, volume* —; the annual meetings of the Society for Information Display; the annual meetings of the IEEE Computer Group, other IEEE meetings which are important as a source of computer literature are the International Convention, National Aerospace Electronics Conference (NAECON), Western Electronics Show and Convention (WESCON), and the Region 6 Conference.

One of the earliest US conferences was the Harvard Symposium, initially held in 1947 and then in 1949, 1955, 1957 and 1961. One of the member societies of AFIPS is the American Documentation Institute (now the American Society for Information Science), whose own annual meeting is a good source for literature on the applications of computers to information science, as are the regular meetings entitled 'Computers and information sciences'.

International meetings held regularly include the very important IFIP congresses held triennially from 1959 onwards, all of which have been published and form a series of basic volumes. The International Association for Analog Computation also holds regular meetings in different countries, under the sponsorship of the national society. The fourth meeting was held in Brighton in 1964 and the proceedings published in Belgium in 1966. The IFIP Administrative Data Processing Group (IAG) also holds many international conferences, including the important ones on file organisation.

The only regular conferences in the UK are the biennial Datafair conferences and exhibitions held by the BCS, and the Infotech state-of-the-art seminars, which attract a wide international audience and are published as comprehensive state of the art reviews. The IEE seems to sponsor, either on its own or jointly, at least three conferences each year which deal with a specialised topic within the computer field. In addition, many of its other conferences seem to include relevant material (*eg* that on 'large steerable aerials' in 1966). Typical of the computer conferences are 'Reliability and maintenance of digital computer systems' (1960) and 'Electronic aids to banking' (1962).

Other countries have their equivalents, *eg* the annual Australian Computer Conferences (now available more easily and abstracted regularly), the NORDSAM conferences, which are held in rotation in the various Scandinavian countries, and the annual meetings of the Canadian Information Processing Society.

For the librarian, and the scientist who wishes to keep up with this important form of communication, there are three interesting problems connected with conferences. These problems are listed below with some methods of overcoming them.

Lack of information about future meetings: This was very serious at one time but there are now a large number of publications giving information about the meetings to be held. Crowell-Collier Macmillan (CCM) publish in two series (one for inside the USA and Canada and one for other countries) *World meetings,* and also *Calls for papers* (both 1968-), which note full details of meetings planned up to three years ahead, with subject and organisation indexes. Many journals publish diaries of national and international meetings, and particularly good sources are *New literature on automation,* and the *Proceedings of the International Association for Analog Computation.* Another source for international meetings is the Union of International Associations' (UIA) *The annual international congress calendar* (1961-), which is supplemented by a list in the union's monthly *International associations.* There are subject and geographical indexes, and details are given, when available, of the projected date and publisher of the proceedings.

Publication fate of papers: This was briefly touched upon in the earlier part of this chapter. A paper by Liebesny delivered at the International Conference on Scientific Information 1958 showed that 48·5 percent of conference papers were not published elsewhere. The way over this problem, if a search has been made without success among the abstracting services, is to check for the existence of preprints via sources such as *World meetings,* or else to contact the author of the paper concerned, either directly or through the sponsoring organisation.

76

Difficulty in tracing published proceedings: There are basically five ways in which the papers presented at a conference may be published: *a*) as preprints; *b*) as complete post-conference proceedings in a journal; *c*) the authors may place the papers individually in a publication of their choice in the normal way; *d*) as a volume of proceedings published by the sponsoring organisation; or *e*) as proceedings published by a commercial publisher. Each of these in turn poses its own problems. The question of preprints has already been covered above. Post-conference journal publication, *b* and *c*, should be traced via the abstracting and indexing journals. The main problem occurs when, as can happen, especially with *c*, the journal publishes the paper with no indication that it was first read at a conference, or the abstracts fail to make this clear, or to index the conference title (again this is more likely with *c*).

The main source of information for sponsor's volume publications, *d*, include national bibliographies and abstracting services. The NLL publishes an *Index of conference proceedings received* (1964-), which has a keyword index to titles. Two very similar US publications are the *Directory of published proceedings* (Interdok, monthly, 1965-), which is published in two series: science, engineering, medicine and technology; and social sciences and humanities. There are cumulative indexes including a five year one. CCM publish a *Current index to conference papers in engineering* (1969-), which has world-wide coverage of 120,000 papers and is also available on magnetic tape. There are similar indexes to chemical and to life science conference papers. The Union of International Associations (UIA) publishes the monthly *Bibliographic current list of papers, reports and proceedings of international meetings* (1961-), which is arranged by UDC and includes those appearing in periodicals. A series of annual volumes is also published.

All of the above sources apply equally to commercially published proceedings, *e*, where the main problem is that the publisher may alter the title or give a more catchy title to what would otherwise be just the ' Proceedings of . . .'.

In 1966, there were 128 conferences which produced a total of 1,966 papers, *ie* 7·9% of the total literature.

These conference papers come from the usual major literature-producing countries *ie* USA 60% (10·9%), USSR 18% (12·2%), UK 8·4% (1%), France 1·5% (4·8%), and West Germany 1·3% (2·2%). In each case, the first figure is the percentage contribution of the country to conference paper production and the second (in brackets) the percentage contribution of conference papers to the country's output.

The coverage by abstracting services was RZK (478), CR (429), STAR (336), CA (310), RZA (302) and CIS (208). It can be seen that even RZK only covered some 25% of the total conference papers and that there is no service which can offer comprehensive coverage. CCA does have better coverage now, but could not be included in these analyses.

12 TRANSLATIONS

THE PROBLEM of the 'foreign language barrier' is no less great in the computer field than in science and technology as a whole. It has been estimated that at least 50 percent of world literature in science and technology is in a language other than English. The proportion is increasing, with Russian rapidly coming into second place after English (ahead of both French and German). As China and the other developing countries become more industrialised, so their share of the literature will increase.

It is important that the computer scientist should be aware of new work that appears in foreign languages—especially Russian, where a great deal of significant work is being carried out in machine translation and information retrieval, to mention only two fields.

A number of solutions have been proposed to break through this language barrier. They include the development of an international language to be learned by scientists, either with or as an alternative to another foreign language (surprisingly little time is needed, at least to get the gist of articles). Foreign language studies have not been pursued to any great extent by scientists in the English speaking countries, and most reliance is still placed on the production of translations. In computer technology, approximately 5 percent of the material appearing in English has been translated (mostly from the Russian).

The production of translations can be divided logically into that done in the originating country and that done in the consuming country.

In the producing country: a) This includes such measures as the US Special Foreign Currency Science Information Program, whereby agricultural produce sold to a country (*eg* Israel, Yugoslavia and Poland) is paid for in the local currency, which is then retained in the purchasing country as a fund to finance translations for the US. This is known as the PL 480 program (from the number of the law which authorised it).

b) Some countries publish widely in English, *eg* Scandinavia (an example here is the journal *BIT*) and Japan. In the latter country about 12 percent of journals appear in English—some only in English, and some with Japanese editions as well.

c) The provision of abstracts in English of the papers in a journal is a very common practice.

d) The publication of national abstracts in English language editions, which have a number of entries for computers and their applications, *eg Japanese periodicals index, Natural sciences section* and *Hungarian technical abstracts*.

In the consuming country : Translation at the consuming end is a very big business. In 1959 the US government translated 51 million words, and it has been estimated that by 1970 some 4,000 million words were translated in the USA each year. As well as a number of commercial firms which exist solely for the production of translations, there are two government agencies (the Joint Publications Research Service, and the Foreign Technology Division, Air Force Systems Command) which produce nothing but translations.

Most translations are made from the Russian language, and a recent count of cover to cover translations and special editions produced the following figures : from Russia 214; Germany 10; China 6; Poland 5; Japan 4; Yugoslavia 3; France, Italy and Czechoslovakia 1 each.

The four main ways in which foreign literature is translated are as follows.

BOOKS

Well over 32,000 books are translated each year from 58 countries. Many of these are scientific and technical. Some of the computer ones are published by commercial publishers (*eg* V M Glushkov *Introduction to cybernetics*. Academic Press, 1966), while the two US government agencies mentioned above also publish a number of translations of books (in fact Glushkov's book was also published in the same year by the Foreign Technology Division, AFSC—an example of duplication which occurs time and time again in the computer field).

ABSTRACT JOURNALS

i) In the USA, especially, there have been large government grants to the major abstracting journals to assist them to acquire and abstract foreign literature.

ii) certain sections of the Russian abstracting journal *Referativyni zhurnal* are translated, *eg Mekhanika* by the Ministry of Technology, and *Kibernetika* (as *Cybernetics abstracts*) (1964-) by Scientific Information Consultants, London.

PERIODICALS

This is probably the major field of activity (as no exact figures are available for ad hoc translations), and it can be subdivided into :

i) Cover to cover translations. In this way the whole of a journal issue is translated, usually on a continuing basis. The advantage is that no discrimination over the inclusion or exclusion of an article is needed once the initial decision to translate the journal has been made.

The disadvantages of cover to cover translations are many, including cost; a time lag of anything up to eighteen months, for which many people cannot afford to wait, and so must commission ad hoc translations in any case; in addition, in spite of the careful selection of journals, many of the articles are not worth the expense of translating. It has also happened that an article has been translated that was itself a translation from the English original.

A list follows of all the journals relating to computers which are either cover to cover translated journals, abstracts of Russian material or regular reviews. The Russian title (if there is one) is given first, followed by all known translations and publishers, dates of publication where known.

Akademiya Nauk SSSR. Izvestiya. Tekhnicheskaya kibernetika (1963-).

Technical cybernetics (JPRS). 1963-.

Engineering cybernetics (Scripta Publishing Corp). 1963-.

Automation express (1958-). Lengthy abstracts of papers published by International Physics Index.

Avtomatika i telemekhanika (1934-).

Automatics and telemechanics (JPRS). 1957-. Abstracts only.

Automation and remote control (Plenum Press). 1956-.

Avtomatika i vychislitel'naya tekhnika (1961-).

Automatic control (Faraday Press). 1967-.

Avtomatyka (1956-).

Automatics (JPRS). 1957-. Abstracts only.

Automation (JPRS).

Soviet automatic control (Scripta). 1968.

Communist Chinese scientific abstracts. Cybernetics, computers and automation technology (1964-). JPRS. Now merged into main series with no subdivisions (1967?).

East European scientific abstracts. Cybernetics, computers and automation technology (1964-). JPRS.

Foreign developments in machine translation and information processing (1961-). JPRS.

Joho shori (1960-).

Information processing in Japan. Information Processing Society of Japan, 1961-. Translation of selected articles only.

Journal of cybernetics (1971-). Scripta. Includes a regular translated papers section.

Kibernetika (1965-).

Cybernetics (JPRS). 1965-.

Cybernetics (Faraday). 1965-.

Nauchno-tekhnicheskaya informatsiya

Automatic documentation and mathematical linguistics (Faraday). 1966-.

Scientific-technical information (JPRS).

Problemy kibernetika (1958-).

Probleme der kibernetik (Akademie Verlag, Berlin).

Problems of cybernetics (Pergamon). 1960-.

Problems of cybernetics (JPRS). 1962-.

Systems theory research (Plenum). 1967-.

Problemy peredachi informatsii (1959-).

  Problems of information transmission (Faraday). 1965-.

  Problems of information transmission (JPRS). 1966-.

Referativnyi zhurnal. kibernetika (1964-).

  Cybernetics abstracts (Scientific Information Consultants). 1964-.

Revista dell'informazione (1970-).

  Information review. 1970-. Complete English translation of Italian papers is included in each issue.

Soviet cybernetics review (1967-). Rand Corporation. Abstracts and translations. Also available as Rand *Memoranda* and AD reports.

Soviet cybernetics technology (1963-1968). Rand Corporation. A most interesting series of reports consisting of translations, reviews and analyses in a variety of areas, including a listing by author of all items in the 1964 *Referativnyi zhurnal kibernetika* (RM-5587, AD666020).

Studii si cercetari de calcul economic si cibernetica economica.

  Economic computation and economic cybernetics studies and research (1966-).

Systems computers controls (Scripta). 1970-. Translations from a number of Japanese journals.

USSR industrial development. Cybernetics, computers and automation technology (JPRS).

USSR scientific abstracts. Cybernetics, computers and automation technology (JPRS). 1964-. Abstracts only.

Vychislitel'nye systemy (1962-).

  Computer elements and systems (JPRS). 1962-.

Zhurnal vychislitel'noi matematiki i matematicheskoi fiziki (1961-).

  USSR computational mathematics and mathematical physics (Pergamon). 1962-.

In view of the disadvantages of cover to cover translations there has been a growing trend away from these towards :

ii) Selective translation of journals. These are made from either one or a number of journals, and the advantage is that all the articles can be aimed at the same level by careful selection of the originals. In addition, the costs and timelags can be reduced. Examples of this type of journal are *Systems computers controls* and *Automatic documentation and mathematical linguistics.*

iii) Abstracts of Russian literature are another way of reducing costs and speeding the flow of information. As well as the translation of *Referativnyi zhurnal kibernetika,* the important ones are *Automation express* and the Joint Publications Research Service series. The merging of all the separately published Chinese sub-series into one publication reflects the recent political climate in that country. Very few scientific periodicals from China seem to be reaching the rest of the world, and the proposed translation of *Acta automatica sinica* seems to have been abandoned. The independent 'Cybernetics, computers and automation technology' sections of both *USSR scientific abstracts* and *East European scientific abstracts* are still being published. The former also includes translations of abstracts from *Referativnyi zhurnal kibernetika.*

AD HOC TRANSLATIONS

These are the most fugitive of all translations. Most organisations make or commission translations at some time or another, and only if they are documentation-minded will they bother to notify one or other of the cooperative groups for translations. The major producers of translations are very good about this, and very often issue their own lists of translations that they have made.

There are in existence a number of information centres relating to translations. They tend to fall into two groups: *a)* indexes from which an enquirer can learn of the existence of a private translation and the source from which it can be borrowed; or *b)* translation depositories which actually collect translations and supply copies of them. There are four major centres in the USA and Europe (as well as others in the German Democratic Republic, Hungary and elsewhere):

i) The Commonwealth Index of Unpublished Scientific and Technical Translations, which is housed at Aslib (with copies in other Commonwealth countries), is a card index arranged by journal citation, which indicates who has made a translation of what. Borrowing can be directly, or if necessary through Aslib, who take care to remove from the copy any indication of the source of the translation. The index has been operating since 1950 and has records of more than 60,000 translations. A success rate of about 12 percent is claimed (which roughly coincides with that reported by the National Science Library, Canada).

ii) The second type of scheme is represented by the National Translations Center (previously the Special Libraries Association (SLA) Translations Pool), which holds well over 100,000 translations. The centre is housed at the John Crerar Library, Chicago, and was started by the SLA in 1953. In 1957 many translations were given by the Library of Congress. In 1958 agreement was reached with the government Office of Technical Services (OTS), whereby the SLA would collect translations made by non-governmental organisations in the USA and abroad, and the OTS would collect government sponsored translations. Each organisation gives copies of their translations to the other.

iii) The other major British source of translations is the National Lending Library, which sponsors cover to cover translations, collects all available cover to cover translations and abstracts, and commissions ad hoc translations. This intake is supplemented by the systematic collection of ad hoc translations of journal articles and books. NLL receives microfilm of translations received at the National Translations Center (7,500 per year), and also sends copies of its translations to NTC. NLL has access also, of course, to all translations announced in *Government reports announcements,* through receipt of microfiche of all reports in this service.

85

The bibliographical control of translated material is fairly good, and there are two major sources which seem to cover comprehensively all reported material.

The National Translations Center issues the *Translations register-index* (1967-), which is published semi-monthly with quarterly and annual cumulations. The ' register ' section contains full bibliographic details of the (non-governmental) translations deposited at NTC; the ' index ' includes these, plus those appearing in *Government reports announcements,* plus any others that NTC knows of.

Since 1968, all government sponsored translations have appeared in *Government reports announcements,* although STAR is better for analytical entries to translations which include different papers, such as the issues of *Technical cybernetics.*

The European Translations Centre at Delft publishes the *World index of scientific translations* (1967-). This has considerable overlap with the *Translations register-index,* and according to Chillag (see below) is unlikely to be of much use to the English speaking scientist. The annual issue, however, does have a complete list of cover to cover and other journals.

Index translationum (UNESCO, annual, 1948-) aims to list books published commercially, translated from and into all language. It is arranged by UDC main classes.

For the period prior to 1968, the major periodical listing translations was *Technical translations* (1959-1967), published by CFSTI, which combined in one index the functions of the *Translations register-index* and *Government reports announcements.*

English language translations made prior to 1966 have been collected into the *Consolidated index of translations into English* which is in two sections—patents, and reports, journals, standards and books. More than 142,000 translations are included.

The major US producer of translations—JPRS, is well served by indexes and an important publishing operation has been created

86

jointly with a commercial publisher, CCM Information Services. Scientific and technical translations are indexed (by country, author, subject and source) in the quarterly *Sci/tech quarterly index* (1970-), whilst all JPRS material appears in the monthly *Transdex,* which includes more than 100,000 items. As well as the indexes (which are also available on magnetic tape), all JPRS documents are available on microfiche or microfilm—over 225,000 pages of translations annually.

An unpublished source of information is a card index at the National Reference Library of Science and Invention of the translations held by them. It is arranged by original journal title, with a separate author sequence for the translations whose original versions are not held by the library.

Guides to translators and services are represented by the UK *Directory of technical and scientific translators and services,* edited by P Millard (Crosby Lockwood, 1968) and the US *Translators and translations: services and sources* edited by F E Kaiser (Special Libraries Association, second edition, 1965).

Finally, this section has been able only very briefly to review sources of translations. A fuller, excellent survey is J P Chillag ' Translations and their guides ' *NLL review* 1(2) April 1971, 46-53, which lists in tabular form and describes the above services and many others.

BIBLIOMETRIC CHARACTERISTICS

More than 1,000 translations were published in 1966, which constituted 4·07% of the literature. 400 of these translations were papers in cover-to-cover translated journals. The majority of translations came, as usual, from the USA 82·7% (which formed 7·8% of the US literature). The other large producers were Israel 7·85% and USSR 3%. Four other countries (France, West Germany, United Kingdom, Holland) contributed just over 1% each and six other countries less than 1% each.

The importance of Israel, which produces translations under the PL480 program, is shown by the fact that translations form 70·2% of the total output of Israel.

The best sources for translations were CIS (58%), STAR (57%), GRA (13·2%) and CA (6·4%). STAR is about the only source for many of the JPRS translations, such as *Technical cybernetics*.

13 ABSTRACTS AND INDEXES IN INFORMATION TRANSFER

THE VOLUME OF scientific publication has grown so much in the last one hundred years that it is obvious that, even within a specialist field such as computing, it is both impossible for any one person to scan all literature appearing, and for any one library to collect all the relevant literature.

The fact that computing is a service technology, which in turn leads to a very high degree of scatter of the literature (see page 12), adds greatly to the problems. Indeed it can be estimated that, to be sure of reading everything relevant to computing, one would have to look at a piece of information regardless of whether it was a two page article or a 500 page book *every three minutes* (assuming an eight hour day and 250 working days in a year).

In order to cope with this situation there have grown up specialist periodicals called abstracting journals (of which indexes are subsets). These present, in condensed form and under convenient headings, relevant information, so that individual workers are able to keep up to date with progress in their own fields without taking up an undue amount of time.

DEFINITION AND FEATURES

Abstracts are summaries of original material which may range from a few words (indicative abstracts, *eg* those in *Computer abstracts*), to several hundred words containing the substance of the original (informative abstracts, *eg* those in *Automation express*). They usually describe the original factually, although some are critical (*eg Computing reviews*). Most abstracts are in fact author-produced and appear in the original publication (60% in *Physics abstracts*, 50% in *Nuclear science abstracts*).

Essential features of an entry in an abstracting journal are : the author's name, article title, bibliographic data (*ie* journal name, volume and part numbers, page numbers and date; or publisher, date, number of pages and possibly a report or patent number); and an abstract. Other information may be included, such as the address or employment of the author, the existence and quantity of illustrations or references, the language of the article, and the identity of the abstractor.

In order that an abstracting journal may be of use in a search for previously published material (retrospective searching), it must be well indexed—author and subject indexes are essential. Other indexes that may be provided are to patent and report numbers, bibliographies, books, sources, acronyms and citations.

Abstracts may be also published as sections of periodicals (*eg* in *IEEE transactions on computers*) or on cards (*eg New literature on automation*) which will fit a standard filing drawer (usually 125mm by 75mm).

Indexes generally give only the author's name, title and bibliographic details of items, arranged systematically. Although in some ways, because no abstract is given, they are less useful than abstracting journals, they are cheaper and quicker to produce. Since scientific titles at least are explicit, it is usually possible to tell from the title alone whether or not an article is likely to be of interest.

Most indexes are not constructed to permit retrospective searching, but are considered as current awareness services. These are rapidly produced media which list the materials either by the source journal or under very broad subject headings (*Current papers on computers and control*). They may be in some cases only reproductions of the contents pages of periodicals (*Contents pages in data processing*). Their great advantage is that they do get information disseminated rapidly, and together with the slower, less selective abstracts or indexes, form a useful two-level information service.

However, the abstracting journal is presented with a set of conflicting requirements and, particularly in view of the growth of the literature, is not conceptually able to fulfil its functions adequately.

The growth of the literature results[1] in:

1 Inadequate coverage by the abstracting services, whose income growth does not match the literature growth. For an example of this see figure 1 on page 95 where it can be clearly seen that most abstracting journals make no attempt at increasing their coverage as the literature increases;

2 Development of a tool whose physical size defeats the goal of alerting users in favour of the alternative goal of the retrospective search. This applies to tools such as *Chemical abstracts*. In general, the computer abstracting journals have avoided this by drastically restricting their coverage;

3 Fragmentation of the abstracting journal into multiple units which reduces opportunities for casual or unplanned cross-disciplinary access, and imposes additional costs to maintain the viability of the fragmentation.

4 A service which not only fails to cover relevant material and overlaps with other services but takes an increasingly long time to include material.

Practical illustration of points 1, 3 and 4 occur in the later discussion of the bibliometric properties of abstracting journals.

The major conflict is thus between the need for comprehensiveness and the need for speed in alerting users to new information.

COMPREHENSIVENESS OF ABSTRACTING JOURNALS
The flow of information can be represented in the following simplified form as:

Primary information $\xrightarrow{\quad 1 \quad}$ abstract journals $\xrightarrow{\quad 2 \quad}$ libraries $\xrightarrow{\quad 3 \quad}$ users

At some stage in this flow there will occur the need to filter out unwanted material. The definition of ' unwanted ' will vary —it may be so because it is on the wrong topic, or written at the wrong level, or in the wrong language, etc.

It is essential that this filtering be done at a stage as close to the user as possible for the following reasons:

a) Consider the situation in which the user is searching for information on a certain topic. At present he must search a number of abstracting services, all of which are selective. He must duplicate his search, accustoming himself to different indexing methods and terms. At the end of this search he cannot be sure whether he has found all the information or, if he has found none, whether this is because there is no information, or because the information has been missed by the services concerned. The result is therefore a considerable expenditure of effort, much of it wasted and with no definite advance assurance of success or failure.

b) The interests and needs of users vary and, indeed, will vary for any one user from time to time, and the attempt to filter the range and level of material, especially at stage 1, will result in user dissatisfaction.

c) Even material which only repeats existing knowledge in a discipline has important uses, especially if written from the point of view of another discipline, or is used as introductory material for, *eg*, managers.

The implications of this therefore are that an abstracting service must be fully comprehensive and must indicate the level or readership of the items which it abstracts.

An additional argument for the comprehensiveness of abstracting journals in computing is the fact that computers are used in the study of *all* other subjects. Computer technology is a service technology, and hence, in common with that other service technology, information science, information on computers will appear among the literature of all other disciplines. In addition, information on applications will appear in ' core ' computer journals, and may be missed by workers in a particular application.

Because of the scattered nature of this information, a comprehensive abstracting journal is an essential part of the process of cross-fertilisation of ideas between *a*) computers and applications areas, and *b*) different applications areas which may be using similar computer techniques.

Finally, the only efficient way of maintaining a constant bibliometric monitor of the information transfer process is by means of a comprehensive abstracting service.

A POSSIBLE ALTERNATIVE

Nevertheless, a totally comprehensive abstracting service for which a case has been implicitly made out above, would, as indicated previously, have disadvantages of bulk and slow coverage of the literature.

A possible alternative to the present inefficient and ineffective structure of abstracting journals would be to promote the comprehensiveness of smaller units, backed up by a centralised and completely comprehensive ' capping agency ' which would only publish abstracting journals in cases where commercial services were not willing to operate. The scheme would need government support, in order to encourage commercial services to expand their coverage and improve speed and indexing.

Each abstracting service would be confined to a small subject area (such as programming, military applications, computer industry). A total of perhaps 20 to 30 would be needed to cover the field completely. Main coverage would be by direct scanning of journals known to be rich in the particular topic (previously identified by a bibliometric study). Secondary coverage to ensure comprehensiveness would be achieved by the capping agency supplying abstracts which it had collected to each individual journal.

The means by which a capping agency could ensure comprehensive coverage of all items of computer literature has been described elsewhere.[2] Each abstracting journal would offer a two-level service of current awareness and retrospective search. They would be able to monitor their own performances by means of statistics supplied by the capping agency, which would also be able to maintain a constant bibliographic monitor on the literature. This would aid the identification of journals which were becoming rich in a particular topic of interest to an abstracting service.

The other functions of the capping agency would be to provide a computer-based search service and an SDI service, and it could also offer comprehensive bibliographics.

While the capping agency and the services it could offer are feasible technically the overall implications of this proposal are such that it could only take place within the context of a national information plan for computer information.

Growth of abstracting services

	CA	CCA	CIS	CJA	CR	EC	LA	RZA	RZK
1953						110			
1954						213			
1955						175			
1956						222			
1957	N/A					229			
1958	N/A					51			
1959	N/A					542			
1960	2503				404	603			
1961	2880				909	651	1194		
1962	3012		2601		2087	629	1459		
1963	3029		2599		1526	616	1286	5031	
1964	3153		2816		1894	513	1680	4840	11473
1965	3409		4442		1933	618	1750	5574	6412
1966	3472		6224		2254	705	2154	4677	9362
1967	3371				2304	616	2975	4976	10691
1968	3416				2549	946	3108	5352	12745
1969	3707	5638		1350	2296	942	2315	5459	12449
1970	3541	9411		2030	2246	932	1619	5883	13786
1971	3441	10027		2261	1962	1006	1589	6701	15330

TABLE 1 : Number of abstracts

BIBLIOMETRIC CHARACTERISTICS

In the ensuing discussion the following abbreviations have been given to each abstracting journal:

94

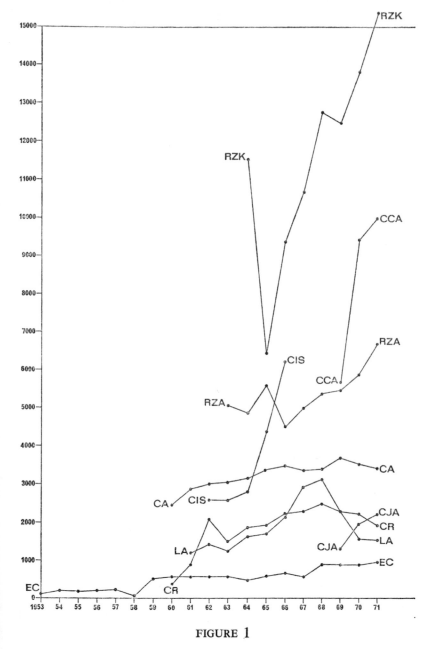

FIGURE 1

CA: *Computer Abstracts;* CCA: *Computer and control abstracts;* CIS: *Computer & information systems;* CJA: *Computing journal abstracts;* CR: *Computing reviews;* EC: *IEEE transactions on computers;* GRA: *Government reports announcements;* LA: *New literature on automation;* RZA: *Referativnyi zhurnal vychislitel'naya tekhnika;* RZK: *Referativnyi zhurnal kibernetika;* STAR: *Scientific and technical aerospace reports.*

A description of each of these services appears in the next chapter. This section discusses the bibliometric properties of these (major) services.

Table 1 and figure 1 illustrate the growth of the services over the years (it should be noted that the figures for CCA relate only to the main computer section—groups 8 and 9 only). We can see immediately that the services have not grown in proportion to the previously discussed explosive growth in the computer literature. Indeed in some cases the quantity of literature has actually declined (*eg* CA, CR and LA from 1969 to 1971). This in itself, without any other evidence, is an indication that the various services are not carrying out their function of abstracting the literature at all well.

Coverage of 1966 literature : The figures given in table 1 are the numbers of abstracts contained in the issues of the abstracting journals with a given date. Table 2, on the other hand, gives the numbers of items of original literature with the publication date of 1966 which appeared in the abstracting journals noted regardless of the actual date of appearance. In some cases, this was as late as December 1968.

CA	CIS	CR	EC	GRA	LA	RZA	RZK	STAR
3391	3833	1718	570	2659	2140	4806	4279	2812

TABLE 2 : 1966 literature contained in abstracting journals

It can be seen that the two general form-oriented services, GRA and STAR, both of which cover only research reports, are as important in terms of the volume of literature contained as most of the major computer abstracting services. In later tables therefore, GRA and STAR will be included in the analyses.

Delay in abstracting: One of the important factors in the evaluation of abstracting services is the length of time it takes for items to appear. Obviously, a good service will report the existence of items as quickly as possible. Table 3 gives the delay (in months) for each service. The first row of figures relates to the 1966 literature. The second row is from two issues in 1971 in an attempt to determine whether the situation has got better or worse in the intervening five years.

	CA	CCA	CIS	CJA	CR	EC	GRA	LA	RZA	RZK	STAR
966	5·24	—	18·6	—	10·15	6·27	5·93	9·62^1	12·5^2	9·2^2	6·34^1
971^3	8·1	5·2	—	0·92	8·6	—	—	3·6	—	—	—

TABLE 3 : Delay in abstracting (months)

Notes: 1 High percentage of items with unknown delay time (LA : 11·2%, STAR : 11·2%).

2 Very high percentage of items with unknown delay time (RZA : 21·6%, RZK : 48%).

3 The 1971 figures are based upon figures from two issues and cover only dated items. No attempt was made (unlike for the 1966 items) to ascertain dates of publication where these were not given.

Coverage of the literature : It has previously been stated that there are at least 40,000 items of computer literature published each year (and the true total is probably much greater than this). From the figure given in tables 1 and 2 it can be seen that the coverage of the literature by these services is very poor. If we restrict ourselves to the 20,268 items actually included in the 1966 study, it can be seen that the largest service (RZA) includes only 23·7% of the literature, whilst the service most commonly available in UK libraries (CA) only covers 16·8%. This is a bad state of affairs, especially when we compare this with chemistry, where more than 300,000 items are abstracted by *Chemical abstracts,* which must cover 90-95 % of the chemical literature.

Overlap of abstracting services : Table 4 presents a matrix of the number of items in common between any pair of services.

	CA	CR	EC	CIS	LA	GRA	RZA	RZK	STAR
CA	3391	719	487	1314	440	798	705	539	495
CR		1718	204	424	256	84	169	332	29
EC			570	462	92	142	153	190	97
CIS				3833	341	984	378	657	1048
LA					2140	16	191	299	4
GRA						2659	33	74	1327
RZA							4806	453	35
RZK								4279	129
STAR									2812

TABLE 4 : Overlap of abstracting services

The large amount of overlap between the major services such as CA, CR, CIS is immediately apparent, as is the heavy dependence of CA and CIS upon GRA, and upon GRA and STAR respectively. Of interest is the very small amount of overlap between the two Russian services (RZA and RZK); this is somewhat surprising. More to be expected is the very small amount of overlap of any of the Western services with the Russian ones.

Table 5 presents this data in a slightly different fashion. It cross tabulates the number of times that an item has been abstracted against each service. If there is for any one service a high percentage of unique items (ie abstracted only once), then this obviously indicates that this service overlaps very little with other services.

We can see from this table that EC has a very low unique item count and a correspondingly high mean. This also shows up in table 4, and reflects EC's habit of concentrating mainly upon items from a few core journals and some reports.

RZA, RZK and LA have high unique counts and correspondingly low means. Although western, LA includes a lot of

98

	CA	CIS	CR	EC	GRA	LA	STAR	RZA	RZK
1	17·8	20·5	38·8	2·28	21·5	56·7	29·9	72	61
2	31·0	32·2	24·4	3·33	43	19·1	42·5	16·8	20·3
3	21·2	22·5	11·75	10·7	21·6	10·7	17·4	3·96	7·83
4	16·4	13·2	8·78	28·1	9·35	6·4	7·48	3·08	4·45
5	7·95	6·73	7·7	29·2	3·23	2·62	2·35	1·62	2·68
6	3·34	2·71	4·77	14·9	0·41	2·2	0·04	1·23	1·73
7	1·74	1·46	2·56	8·4	0·375	1·49	0	0·79	1·21
8	0·45	0·39	0·7	2·46	0	0·51	0	0·27	0·327
9	0·15	0·13	0·28	0·88	0	0·094	0	0·104	0·17
Mean	2·9	2·7	2·5	4·7	2·3	1·9	2·1	1·5	1·8

TABLE 5 : Number of times abstracted (percentages)

European literature from business journals which are not touched by, *eg,* CA. RZK has a lower unique item count than RZA because it includes more western literature.

The relatively low unique counts for GRA and STAR are a reflection of the fact that GRA is the service published by the reports clearinghouse and thus acts as a source journal for many other services (including STAR). It is thus an essential service for any other service which wishes to include US report literature. The difference between them is because STAR is used somewhat less as a source journal.

Country of publication: Table 6 answers the question of where the abstracting journals draw their literature from. Is there a national bias? Included in table 6 are all countries which contribute more than 1% to the content of any abstracting journal, and also the percentage figure for the contribution of these countries to the literature as a whole.

It can be seen at once that there definitely is a national bias in abstracting services, and that there is a western bias and even parochialism amongst some services.

National bias can be seen in the American services (CR, CIS, EC, GRA and STAR), in the Dutch service (LA), and in one Russian service (RZK), where in each case the 'home' country's per-

	ALL	CA	CIS	CR	EC	GRA	LA	STAR	RZA	RZK
Austria	0·39			1·05						
Belgium	0·8						1·4		2·4	2·5
Czechoslovakia	1·5						4·55			
Denmark	0·29			1·63						
E Germany	1·5								3·5	1·44
France	2·95		1·2			1·01	1·92		4·8	3·5
Holland	1·38			1·98			6·35			
Hungary	0·65						6·6			1·08
Israel	0·56	1·0								
Italy	0·78			1·28					11·5	1·35
Japan	3·85			1·16						4·3
Jugoslavia	0·31						1·17			
Poland	0·72									1·56
Rumania	0·56									1·24
Switzerland	0·57						1·31		1·1	
UK	8·15	11·2	9·45	8·45	14·2	1·68	12·3	3·1	6·7	6·45
USA	53	79·5	77	72·3	79·5	91·5	39·7	77·5	38·3	25·4
USSR	14·2		3·2	1·05				8·8	20·8	42
W Germany	5·5	4·2	3·52	5·65	4·03	1·32	21·2	1·53	3·9	3·6

TABLE 6: National origin of abstracts (percentages)

centage has been greatly raised above its percentage inter-nationally.

Western bias can be seen among the US and UK services, where countries other than US, UK and possibly West Germany are virtually ignored. Parochially, the US and UK services draw from a much more restricted set of countries than do LA, RZA and RZK. CR is better in this respect than the other US services.

CONTROL OF ABSTRACTING SERVICES

If any specific abstracting service is required which covers com-puter applications in a particular field, or if more general ser-vices are needed to extend the coverage of an information service, then there are two major lists published. Both of these give world coverage, but both are very incomplete and they must be used together. It is believed that the two organisations concerned will produce a joint list (an obvious rationalisation) in the future. Perhaps we will then have a truly complete inter-national list of abstracting services.

The most recent of the two was published by the International Federation for Documentation in 1969. It is called *Abstracting services,* and appears in two volumes: volume1—Science, tech-nology, medicine and agriculture; volume 2—Social sciences and humanities. The main section is an alphabetic list of ab-stracting services only (no indexing services are included), giving information on publisher, date of starting, frequency, price, number of abstracts, length of abstract, delay (but these figures should be compared with those given in this chapter), coverage of forms of material, how arranged, indexes and sub-ject scope. There are also a UDC index to titles, a four-language subject index to UDC numbers, and a country index listing titles.

This service is useful but should be treated with considerable caution, as there are some very surprising omissions in our area, *eg Computing reviews* and *IEEE transactions on com-puters.* This tends to throw doubt upon the value and complete-ness of the entries.

It is necessary therefore to use also a much older service which also includes indexing services and probably is more complete.

This is *A guide to the world's abstracting and indexing services in science and technology* (National Federation of Science Abstracting and Indexing Services, 1963). More than 1,800 services (including journals with abstracts sections) are listed, arranged alphabetically by title, with a country index, and UDC and alphabetic subject indexes. The information given is very similar to the FID guide.

New abstracting services can be discovered in the same way as new periodicals, *eg* through *New serial titles* and *British union catalogue of periodicals*. In addition *FID bulletin* updates the FID guide each month, and the information science newsletters, such as *Information*, are good sources to scan.

REFERENCES
1 Carter, L F *et al*: *National document handling systems for science and technology*. Wiley, 1967. 344p.
2 Pritchard, A: Computers, bibliometrics and abstracting services. *Research in librarianship* (15) Sept 1970, 94-99.

14 COMPUTER ABSTRACTS AND INDEXES

MAJOR SERVICES: *Computer abstracts* (UK, monthly, 1960-) continues *Computer bibliography* (1958-1959) and covers mostly periodicals, research reports and patents, together with some books and the major conferences. The abstracts are indicative and arranged by means of a subject classification consisting of the following headings: general computer theory; logic design; artificial intelligence; pattern recognition; mathematics; techniques; programming; system design; digital circuits and components; data storage; input-output; data transmission; specific digital computers; analog computers; hybrid and other computers; education and personnel; applications (aerospace, business, chemical, control-general systems, control-production and process, education, electronics, engineering-electrical, engineering-mechanical, engineering-structural, information retrieval, linguistics, medical, military, mining, physics, transport, miscellaneous); books.

Most abstracts are published on applications, mathematics, hardware and programming. Coverage of US and UK patents is believed to be fairly complete, but less than one third of the research reports available from scanning *Government reports announcements* are included. Other major gaps include theses (not covered at all) and books (poorly covered). In common with all other services, CA makes no attempt to include manufacturers' literature.

Indexes appear in each monthly issue (author, patent and a short keyword index), and in an annual index issue which contains author, patent (*ie* corporate author) and subject. Good points about the indexes are the inclusion, in the subject index, of patent and book indicators after the abstract number, and of general headings such as bibliographies and conferences. Bad points are the small number of indexes, the fact that the author index does not include corporate authors, and the quality of the subject index. The annual index also lists the periodicals referred to (about 150 of them), with details of publishers.

Computer and control abstracts (UK, monthly, 1969-; formerly *Control abstracts,* 1966-1968) is published by the Institution of Electrical Engineers as part of their *INSPEC* (Information Services in Physics Electrotechnology Computers and Control) system. It is, so far, the only computer abstracting service to be mechanised. It is computer typeset and available on magnetic tape to subscribers for in-house searching.

The abstracts are indicative, and arranged according to a numerical classification scheme which covers control and computing. The main sections of interest are: 6 Systems and control theory (containing at the first level of breakdown: mathematical techniques; systems and cybernetics; control theory), 8 Computer programming and applications (containing: general computer topics; numerical analysis; programming systems, languages and processors; file organisation and business handling; information science and documentation; administrative data processing; other computer applications) and 9 Computer systems and equipment (containing: computer metatheory and switching theory; logic elements and circuits; logic-design and digital techniques; digital storage devices and techniques; computer peripherals; digital computers and systems; analog computers and computation).

The majority of abstracts appears on scientific and engineering applications and computer hardware. The journals scanned are still to a great extent orientated to the other INSPEC services and, hence, coverage of electrical, electronics and communications applications is particularly good. Coverage of business applications, the computer industry, etc is not yet as good; that of US and UK patents and conferences is good; of books is fairly good; and of reports and manufacturers' literature very poor, although some manufacturers' conferences (*eg* DECUS) are included.

A recent statement (in IEE catalogue 1971) claimed that in 1971 the INSPEC services as a whole would scan nearly 2,000 periodicals, 5,000 theses, 600 reports, 9,000 patents, 1,200 books and 500 conference proceedings.

CCA is well endowed with indexes. Each monthly issue contains an author index, a supplementary list of journals (*ie* new ones added to those scanned), a bibliography index, a book index, a conference index, a patent index (by patent number) and a report index (by corporate author). All these are cumulated six-monthly and a subject index added. Cumulative indexes are also produced—the one for CCA covering the period 1966-1968.

As well as being available on magnetic tape, CCA has been obtainable on microfiche since January 1970. INSPEC also offer an SDI service based upon CCA. Profiles for this service, which notifies subscribers weekly on 6 × 4 in. cards of documents matching the profile, are built up using Boolean logic operating upon free-index terms, authors' journal names, languages, CCA classification codes and treatment codes (*eg* theoretical or bibliography). Standard profiles are constructed for certain subject areas in which there is considerable interest and growth, and are available on cards as INSPEC *Topics*. These cost somewhat less than the specially tailored SDI service and cover such areas as CAD, memory devices and applications in power engineering.

Computing reviews (US, monthly, 1960-) is published by the ACM, and relatively unusual in that generally it contains true reviews, *ie* signed and critical (and occasionally several pages long).

The abstracts are arranged by a numerical classification scheme which divides into seven sections: general topics and education; computing milieu; applications (natural sciences, engineering, social and behavioural sciences, humanities, management data processing, artificial intelligence, information retrieval, real time systems); programming; mathematics of computation; design and construction; analog computers. The CR categories are appended to articles in the ACM *Journal* and *Communications*. The scheme has been used in some libraries and program libraries to classify records of documents and

105

programs, and has been slightly altered recently to take account of changes in computer topics.

The majority of abstracts is published on mathematics, applications and programming. Coverage is good of books, journal literature, conferences and US theses; a few research reports are included.

Each monthly issue contains an author index, which is cumulated in the December issue. Subject indexes are contained in a series of computer produced permuted indexes covering 1960-1963, 1964-1965, 1966, 1967, 1968 and 1969. The 1960-1963 index contained a KWIC index, bibliography and author index. The 1964-1965 index contained these plus a section in which entries were arranged by CR categories. The annual indexes have the same features as the 1964-1965 one, with the addition of a reviewer index. The material included is expanded by the addition of two classes of material which have not appeared in CR, *viz* (*i*) older and fringe material which would not, now, appear and (ii) material which, because of the delay in reviewing, will appear in the next year's CR.

A unique feature of CR is the appearance of good bibliographies, *eg* real-time computer systems (August 1970) or formal language theory and automata theory (July 1970).

New literature on automation (Holland, monthly, 1961-) is compiled by the Studiecentrum voor Informatica with the co-operation of other organisations in Holland, France, Germany and Latin America. The abstracts are indicative and in either English, French, German or Spanish, with one-line summaries in the other three languages.

The abstracts are arranged by a very detailed classification scheme, and each one has, in addition to the LA class number, some keywords (usually not more than two) and a UDC number. A loose inset to each monthly issue lists forthcoming conferences, and a list of the periodical issues indexed is also included.

The indexes provided are monthly subject (by class number) and author (which also includes titles of anonymous articles). The subject index, at one time, was quite unique in that additional items were included under the appropriate class numbers, which did not carry abstracts. No annual indexes are produced, but there are cumulative indexes (author and subject) covering 1961-1964 and 1965-1968.

Each abstract (apart from items appearing in the index only) is also issued on 125mm × 75mm cards, so that a comprehensive cumulative file can be built up. There are plans to mechanise the production of LA under the title of *Excerpta informatica,* which would provide tapes, a printed service, SDI and retrospective searching.

LA is especially strong on business automation and Western European periodicals. Its areas of weakness include non-periodical literature, generally and in terms of subjects—computer theory, hardware and detailed software material. It does manage to include a lot of manufacturers' literature, and is unique among the abstracting journals in this respect.

Computing journal abstracts (UK, weekly, 1969-) is a newcomer to the field. Originally published as an internal bulletin for the National Computing Centre Ltd, it was sold publicly in 1971.

The indicative abstracts are arranged not by a fixed classification scheme, but in an *ad hoc* format depending upon the material abstracted each week. In general, however, material on the computer industry appears first, followed by education, hardware and peripherals, programming and applications.

The abstracts are arranged on the page so that they could be cut up to form 125mm × 75mm slips. Each carries one or more Studiecentrum classification numbers. In this way, multi-faceted topics can be specified somewhat more precisely than in LA.

A six-monthly subject index (in class number order) has been published, and it is intended that this should cumulate. NCC are carrying out experiments on these abstracts with a view to offering an SDI service which will eventually cover not only literature, but also programs, hardware and background information. This information will be indexed in a standard fashion, using the NCC thesaurus of computing terms. In terms of quantity and delay in abstracting, this new service compares very well with the others.

Computer and information systems is the last in a long line of abstracting services published by the Cambridge Communications Corporation in the United States. They originally published *Computer abstracts on cards* (1959-), which was arranged by a detailed formal classification scheme, with notation. In 1960 the cards were collected into loose leafbook form, and all abstracts were issued annually as *Cumulative computer abstracts,* even after the card service ceased in 1964. *Information processing journal* (1962-) was started as an updating service to the annual volumes, although, since indexes to it are published, it is more generally used as an abstracting journal in its own right. The name was changed to *Computer and information systems,* with volume 6, number 1 in 1969. *Cumulative computer abstracts* has ceased publication as looseleaf volumes and now appears as hard or soft backed books on particular areas of computing, *eg* computer software. These cumulate abstracts in the abstracting journal, although, since they are not at all well indexed, the journals are still needed.

The publication schedules and coverage of this journal and range of publications have always been very much subject to variation (this is reflected in the long delay time of 18·6 months in 1966). With the issue of volume 7, number 9, which arrived in the UK in spring 1970, the abstracting journal temporarily ceased. It restarted in mid 1971. Volumes of *Cumulative computer abstracts* have appeared in this period, however.

These problems, which seem to have been exacerbated by a change in the firm's management structure, are *most* regrettable because the quality of this journal has always been of the highest. Coverage has been good—especially of research reports, indexing has been excellent and unsurpassed by any other service, and the subject arrangement and cross-referencing has been completely clear and helpful. The classification scheme has varied from issue to issue. The major

108

change has been the bringing of mathematics, *OR*, statistics and information theory to the front.

The major Russian abstracting service is *Referativnyi zhurnal avtomatika telemekhanika i vychislitel'naya tekhnika* (1963-), a part only of the world's largest and most comprehensive abstracting service. This service is divided into sixty one separate series (the above being one) which may be subdivided, *eg* the computer section *Vychislitel'naya tekhnika* is available separately. The coverage is especially strong on Russian, East European and Asian literature and is of books, reports, patents (US, UK, USSR, France, Germany, Sweden, Austria, Czechoslovakia, Japan and others) and conferences. In terms of subjects, coverage tends to be concerned with computer science, *ie* hardware, programming, etc.

The abstracts are arranged in a standard subject grouping and have UDC numbers appended. Author and subject indexes are published. The former is divided into two parts—one in Roman script, the other in Cyrillic, according to the language of the original.

The other important Russian service is *Referativnyi zhurnal kibernetika* (1964-), which covers ' the theory and application of logical systems, automatic control theory, information theory, operations research and mathematical economics, computer theory and applications, application of mathematics and cybernetics in biology, psychology and mathematical linguistics ' (*Cybernetic abstracts*). This service is translated into English— partly as *Cybernetics abstracts* (1964-) and partly (the section on mathematical statistics) in *USSR scientific abstracts, cybernetics, computers and automation technology*.

Cybernetics abstracts gives complete translations of East European, Russian and Asian literature, and author, title and bibliographic citations for West European and American literature. It is an important service because of the insight it can give into the Russian developments and also (and this is true of *Referativnyi zhurnal avtomatika*) because the Russian services are so wide ranging that they include a great deal of Western material excluded elsewhere. Monthly author indexes appear in *Cybernetics abstracts,* and monthly and annual author and classified subject indexes to *Referativnyi zhurnal kibernetika.*

OTHER COMPUTER SERVICES

This section deals with a variety of secondary services reporting on computer literature—indexes, smaller (quantitatively) abstracting journals and some in applications areas.

IEEE transactions on computers has included a section of abstracts since 1953. While not large in number, they nevertheless provide a very rapid survey of the more academic and research orientated periodicals and reports. In the past the abstracts have been compiled by Cambridge Communications Corporation, while now they are compiled by Information Associates, who still adhere to the broad categories of the Cambridge classification scheme. Naturally, coverage is very selective, but even in the 1966 literature, when the abstracts were compiled by the compilers of CIS, they did not overlap completely. Indexes provided in each issue are author, subject and identifier. The latter covers acronyms, computers, named numerical (or other) methods, etc. The indexes are cumulated annually in the December issue. For a relatively small abstracts section, there has always been a very high percentage of index entries.

Current papers on computers and control (1966-) is a monthly indexing service which provides quick access to the literature. It is arranged by the same classification scheme as CCA, and does not give an abstract. The delay in publishing material is reduced to 5·1 months as compared with the 5·2 months of CCA.

Data processing digest (1955-) presents about 200-300 lengthy abstracts each year, selected from a wide range of computer and business publications. The abstracts are good ones and concentrate upon important contributions in the administrative data processing area. Also included are notes of new books and new products and a conference list. A unique feature of this service is that usually the abstracts are preceded by an

110

article which reviews a particular area of administrative data processing. Frequently these articles form a series of about a dozen, which are then collected into book form. A recent example was the series entitled ' The EDP people problem '.

Specialised abstracting journals are now being published, such as *Language and automation* (1970-), an international effort to cover literature dealing with the interfaces of linguistics, formal linguistic theory (including abstract languages), applications of computers to linguistics, mechanical translation, statistical linguistics, languages, CAI (particularly applied to language studies), linguistic aspects of computing, information science, humanities applications and related fields. Approximately 1,600-1,700 abstracts will appear in one year. Each quarterly issue has subject and author indexes.

Another specialist service is *Computers in medicine abstracts*.

Abstracting services covering programs (such as *Computer program abstracts* and *ICP quarterly*) are dealt with fully in chapter 22.

An unique approach to abstracting has been adopted by the *Quarterly bibliography of computers and data processing* (Applied Computer Research, 1971-). Recognising that literature can become out of date quite quickly as a result of rapid technological change, this service cumulates literature for three to four years. In the April issue each year entries from the fourth prior year are eliminated, and the content will build up throughout the year until the January issue, which will cover the full four years. The publishers also recognise that some topics will require literature searches going back in time more than four years, but in view of the market that they are aiming at, this policy is reasonable and well thought-out.

The audience is primarily those individuals engaged at the practising end of the computer profession, *ie* users, consultants, etc. Highly research orientated and the more esoteric and academic literature will not be found in the bibliography. The statement of editorial policy in the issue for April 1971 is clear, lays down exactly what is included and what is not and could well be a model for other services.

The entries are arranged under subject headings (which are listed and defined) and the new entries for each quarter are asterisked. The main body of service is preceded by a section highlighting significant papers published in the quarter. A list of publishers is also included.

Anbar abstracts has recently started a separate section called *Accounting and data processing abstracts* which includes about 600 abstracts per year on the applications of computing to business. In this section are collected all computer items abstracted by Anbar even if they appear in one of the other sections. Anbar offer a tear-sheet library and translate some of the foreign language material.

Finally, many of the manufacturers' libraries produce abstracting services which can be valuable in covering the literature. While these are not generally available, most librarians would treat sympathetically a request to be placed upon the mailing list (unless of course the bulletin contained company confidential material or the request came from a competitor).

APPLICATIONS AREAS

Computer technology, being a service technology, appears in the literature of virtually all other disciplines, and hence in their abstracting services. It is possible here to give only a brief selection of the more important ones which are likely to include considerable computing literature. Specific services must be searched for in the guides listed in the section on Control.

The most prolific areas are undoubtedly adjacent disciplines such as mathematics and control science. *Mathematical reviews* is the largest and most comprehensive service in this field and covers fully areas of metatheory and logic, as well as numerical analysis. For control systems we must turn to the control chapters of *Computer and control abstracts*.

Another INSPEC service which contains material on the electronic fundamentals of computing is *Electrical and electronics abstracts*, which, together with *Electronics abstracts journal*, covers this field well.

The applications of computers to plant and process control are numerous, and *Chemical abstracts* virtually abstracts this area completely, although there are also specialist services, in particular chemical technologies such as petroleum, pulp and paper, etc.

The major source for literature on the related topic of operational research (many of the techniques of which are impossible without the computer) is *International abstracts of operational research*.

The major general science and engineering services are very useful sources. The important *Engineering index*, which covers about 2,246 journals, as well as many important scientific and engineering conferences, appears monthly and annually. The material is arranged under subject headings, with an author index. *Pandex*, a rather similar service which claims to cover more than 2,400 journals, 6,000 books and 35,000 reports, appears biweekly and is available also on magnetic tape and microfiche.

The French *Bulletin signalétique* is a multi-subject abstracting service in over twenty series. Section 1 (Mathématiques pures et appliquées) has a large section on computers, with good coverage of European (and particularly French) literature.

Most countries have national abstracting or indexing services, such as *British technology index*, which will include more minor journals not included in larger services. They also have the advantage of being cross-disciplinary.

An inter-disciplinary service from the Institute of Scientific Information is based upon citations appended to papers. The basic service is *Science citation index*, which collects over a million citations each year from more than 2,500 journals. Other services are ASCA (Automatic Science Citation Alert)— an SDI service based upon citations and keywords in the source or cited literature (selection can also be based upon author organisations, author names, journal names).

113

15 BOOKS AND HANDBOOKS

IN SPITE of the rapid growth of the scientific journal and of the research report, scientific books have by no means been left behind in the increasing volume of publications. Their relative importance has certainly declined, but they still make their own contribution to the chain of scientific communication and information storage, most particularly in that they synthesise material widely scattered elsewhere. Although, as a result of modern methods of printing, some books may be able to contain results of original research work, on the whole they remain repositories of what is best in current theory and practice at the time of the book's writing (which may be as long as two years before publication).

Books offer convenient starting points for literature searches, for they furnish information in a form responsive to quick reference, and guide the reader back, by means of bibliographies, to the important original literature. When a new field is studied, books provide the most convenient way of charting its development and structure, as well as identifying the significant original literature.

Many different types of books are published, and such things as directories, data compilations, annual reviews and bibliographies are or can be books. I have included in this chapter one class of books which deserve, if not a complete chapter, at least a significant section within one.

HANDBOOKS

Handbooks are large works which cover a chosen field comprehensively and in considerable detail. The difference between a handbook and an advanced textbook can be unclear at times; it could be dependent upon the number of pages or on the

114

overall comprehensiveness. Huskey and Korn, in the work cited below, describe a handbook as a volume in which, in their own field, ' sufficient detail is presented so that anyone competent in the field can proceed to construct a computer, or, handling a computer, can proceed to use it '.

The major English language handbooks are all American in origin. The oldest, but still worth including, is the *Handbook of automation, computation and control,* edited by E M Grabbe, S Ramo and D E Wooldridge (Wiley, 1958-61). Volume two is devoted to ' Computers and data processing ' (volume one to ' Control fundamentals ' and volume three to ' Systems and components ') and is organised into six sections: computer terminology (very full); digital computer programming; use of digital computer and data processors; design of digital computers; design and applications of analog computers; unusual computer systems.

Computer handbook, edited by H D Huskey and G A Korn (McGraw Hill, 1962), covers the components, theory and applications of analog (sections 1-9) and digital (sections 10-20) computers. The sections are well organised, and there are outlines of the structure at the head of each section.

A more recent work is *Digital computer users' handbook,* edited by M Klerer and G A Korn (McGraw Hill, 1967). This has thirty one essays of varying levels grouped into four areas: programming, numerical techniques, statistical methods and computer applications. In common with most of this type of work, there are good bibliographies.

A unique series of publications which, I think, fall into this class are the Infotech *State of the art reports.* They contain distillations and analyses of the topic, transcripts of papers given at the State of the art lectures, additional invited papers, a bibliography and index. The 1971 series consists of eleven reports on such topics as on the fourth generation, giant computers, real time, software engineering, etc.

The Handbook of data processing management (Auerbach, 1970-1971) covers the entire area of the ' system life cycle ' from conception, through analysis, design programming, installation, operation to cessation. In six volumes and with 2,000 pages, it obviously represents a vast amount of effort.

In most countries of the world national bibliographies are now produced which, at their best, contain details of all published books and pamphlets. Most of the bibliographies depend on some form of deposit law, whereby copies of everything published must be deposited at the national library, and the bibliography is then compiled from the deposited material.

National bibliographies include, to a greater or lesser extent, new periodicals, research reports, the more substantial trade literature, conference proceedings, theses, standards, annual reviews, translations and bibliographies; but for lists which cover each of these materials separately, see those sections dealing with their control, at the ends of the relevant chapters.

The principal methods of learning of the appearance of new books, apart from national bibliographies, is through new literature sections and book reviews in periodicals (although the latter may appear a long time after publication); abstracts and indexes, especially those in *Computing reviews* and *Referativnyi zhurnal*; publishers' announcements.

Ideally, a national bibliography should include *every* piece of printed or duplicated material which is published, except that which is security classified together with all maps, theses, microforms, gramophone records, films etc. In fact, complete listing of these materials in one journal is rare, and there are usually separate lists for non-printed forms of communication such as films.

When it comes to searching, it is important to distinguish between those bibliographies which are based on the influx of material to a national library as a result of legal deposit laws (referred to as *official bibliographies,* even though they may not be actually produced by the national library), and those which are based on some form of voluntary notification, usually to a trade or independent service (referred to as *trade bibliographies*).

This section considers some of the more important national bibliographies, and comments on *a)* bibliographies of current

116

material and *b)* guides to material which is in print at any given time.

England

a) i) The official bibliography is the weekly *British national bibliography* (1950-), which is based on publications received on deposit at the British Museum. Coverage of both trade and non trade books and pamphlets is very good. Certain classes of material are excluded, but for computer literature purposes, these are unimportant (apart from trade literature). A classified arrangement is adopted, and the subject entries in the combined author-title-series-subject index are very satisfactory. The index cumulates monthly, and the whole work three, six and nine monthly, annually and five yearly.

ii) The most complete trade publication is Whitaker's *Cumulative book list* (1924-), based on the weekly entries in *The Bookseller, The Bookseller* lists cumulate monthly, and the *Cumulative book list* does so three, six and nine monthly, annually and two or three yearly. Arrangement is alphabetical by author, title and catchword subject—not so useful as BNB. Entries however appear more quickly than in BNB. Coverage of trade publications is good—of non trade not so good as BNB.

b) i) *British books in print* (annual, 1967-; formerly *Reference catalogue of current literature* irreg, 1874-) is compiled by Whitaker's, and the arrangement and coverage is the same as the *Cumulative book list,* with author entries in volume 1 and title/catchword in volume 2.

USA

a) i) *Cumulative book index* (monthly, 1898-) is the major trade publication, and aims to cover *all* books published in English throughout the world. It is strongest on US and on trade publications, and good on non trade but by no means complete. Arrangement is with authors, titles, subjects, editors etc in one alphabetical sequence. It cumulates two or three monthly, six monthly, annually, two and five yearly. It is a very useful list.

ii) Mention should be made here of the subject edition of the *National union catalog,* which, because of the wide acquisitions policy of the Library of Congress and the 400 other libraries which it covers, and because it is published quickly with accurate subject headings, is one of the most useful lists for world, as well as US literature. This work is described more fully in the section on libraries and their catalogues (page 175).

b) Currently available books are listed in *Books in print* and the *Subject guide to books in print* (both annual, Bowker). The first named has two sequences—one of authors and the other of titles. The latter lists books by alphabetical subject headings with a considerable section on computers.

France

a) i) The official bibliography is the weekly *Bibliographie de la France* (1811-), which arranges in classified sequence books, pamphlets etc received on deposit at the Bibliothèque Nationale. There is an annual author and title index.

ii) The most useful listing is the trade bibliography *Biblio* (monthly, 1933-), which lists authors, titles, and subjects in one alphabetical sequence and cumulates annually. It aims to include all French language books published, not only in France, but in Canada, Switzerland, and other French speaking countries.

Germany

Germany, reflecting the political division, has two national bibliographies, both of which claim to include all German language books published, and which are very similar.

Deutsche bibliographie (Federal Republic) is published weekly and arranges books in twenty six classes. Indexes are author and catchword subject, which culminate half yearly, and (appearing very late) five yearly.

Deutsche nationalbibliographie (DDR) is published in two sections: Reihe A (weekly) lists trade material, and Reihe B (semimonthly) covers theses, institutional publications, off-prints and government publications. Both are arranged in twenty four classes and both have author and catchword subject indexes, which cumulate quarterly and annually.

USSR

There are a variety of sources for new Russian books, of

118

which two published by the All-Union Book Chamber in Moscow should be mentioned:

Knizhnaya letopis', a weekly classified list with a quarterly author index, and *Yezhegodnik knigi SSSR: sistematiches ukazatel'*, a half yearly classified list cumulating the section ' Books of the week ' in *Novye knigi*.

The bibliography by Gros (see chapter 17) is a useful source for 1965-1966 Russian literature.

SCIENTIFIC BOOKS

There are a number of sources specifically for scientific books. Two important ones are:

Aslib book list (monthly) which arranges selected and recommended books by UDC order. Books are reviewed by specialists, brief annotations and an indication of level being given. There are monthly and annual author and subject indexes. Titles included are usually restricted to books in English but occasionally a foreign work will be included.

The second important source is the monthly list of new scientific books which is published in the periodical *Nature*.

One other useful, fairly recent, service, from Britain, is the annual *Technical books in print* (1964-5-), which is produced by Whitaker's, the publishers also of *British books in print*, and arranges its contents by author within fairly detailed subject groups, which follow broadly the UDC classification.

BIBLIOMETRIC CHARACTERISTICS

839 books were published in the field in 1966, which produced 2,646 individually authored texts (this of course includes 1,474 conference papers). Books constituted 3·35% of the literature.

Countries most prolific in book publishing were the United States 37% (2·9%), Russia 27·5% (8%), UK 11·7% (5·9%), West Germany 7·3% (5·5%), Holland 4·8% (14·3%), and France 2·9% (4%). In each of these cases the first figure represents the percentage of book production and the second (in brackets) the percentage of that country's output.

The most prolific sources of book information among the abstracting journals were LA 34·5% (13·5%), RZK 30·8% (6%), CR 24% (12·2%), RZA 15·6% (2·7%). Again, the first figure represents the percentage of book production and the second that of abstracts in an abstracting journal.

16 ANNUAL REVIEWS

ANNUAL REVIEWS are a comparatively late addition to the means by which the output of technical literature is controlled. Publication of annual reviews on any scale started in the late 1950's, and their production is mainly concentrated in the hands of a few large publishing firms (Academic Press, Pergamon Press, for example).

The importance of the medium lies in the fact that annual reviews are intermediate in form and purpose between journals and books. They can take an overall look at segments of a subject field, and, ideally, the articles which they contain should indicate the significant new work which has been reported during the year, and integrate it into the existing pattern of knowledge within the field. The scope of the articles should be planned so that the whole of the chosen field can be covered, and the depth of this treatment inevitably means that the reviews contain copious references to the general and special literature of the subject.

Advances in computers (Academic Press) was started in 1960, and contains well documented review articles upon areas of current interest in computers. The emphasis is on practical applications, *eg* weather prediction, machine translation and information retrieval, and on programming rather than on hardware. Each volume contains the contents list of all the previous volumes.

The *Annual review in automatic programming* was also started in 1960, and was edited by Richard Goodman of the Automatic Programming Information Centre, Brighton (UK) College of Technology. It reports on work done on languages, and is perhaps more an annual journal than an annual review. After some vicissitudes following the death of Goodman, it is now being published again on a regular basis by Pergamon Press.

The latest annual review is edited by J T Tou and called *Advances in information systems science* (Plenum, 1969-). It contains reviews of mainly theoretical areas such as pattern recognition, learning systems and computer theory.

Each of the annual reviews so far mentioned has had no consistency of content from year to year. They have simply chosen interesting areas and included them. The alternative approach is provided by the *Annual review of information science and technology* (1966-), which has a fairly consistent set of subject headings, and reviews the significant related literature. Although primarily orientated to the needs of librarians and information scientists, it has a heavy computer bias, with chapter headings such as computer technology, communications technology, library automation, management information systems and information systems in state and local government.

Other annual reviews which have interest for the computer field are *Methods in computational physics* (Academic Press, 1963-) and *Advances in control systems* (Academic Press, 1964-).

Methods in computational physics covers much the same area as *Journal of computational physics*. It is interesting in that each volume covers a specific topic: volume 1 (1963) statistical physics; volume 2 (1963) quantum mechanics; volume 3 (1964) fundamental methods in hydrodynamics; volume 4 (1965) applications in hydrodynamics; volume 5 (1966) nuclear particle kinematics; volume 6 (1966) nuclear physics; volume 7 (1967) astrophysics.

To learn of new annual reviews which may be published in the future (and there will undoubtedly be more of this type of publication), all of the sources for scientific books mentioned in chapter 15 apply. In addition, annual reviews in all fields are listed in the second edition of *List of annual reviews of progress in science and technology* (Paris, UNESCO, 1969), which is a subject list of annual reviews with details of publisher, date of first volume and date and price of latest volume. In 1965 the NLL published *Some current review series,* which is an alphabetical listing only of about 270 review publications.

Many journals publish review articles and bibliographies either regularly or occasionally. *VDI zeitschrift* (West Germany) regularly has articles of the kind and often they deal with computers or a related topic. *Industrial and engineering chemistry* (USA) has issued an article each December on process control, which reviews the new literature of the past year.

An American yearbook which reviews the computer field at an introductory level is the *Computer yearbook and directory* (American Data Processing Inc, 1966-), which, prior to 1966, was known as the *Data processing yearbook* (1962-1965), and as the *Punched card annual* (1952-1961). Emphasis now is entirely on computers, and as well as an extensive reference section described elsewhere, the articles survey current development under the heads humanities; state of the art; hardware; software; data communications; technique and industries.

17 BIBLIOGRAPHIES

BIBLIOGRAPHIES are lists of references to other literature. The references may be to any single type, or to all types of materials, and may be limited by specific subjects (usually), period of time, country, etc.

It is apparent that abstracts and indexes (chapter 14) are also bibliographies according to this definition, but this chapter is only concerned with bibliographies which are published either as books and pamphlets, or as parts of books, or as papers in journals.

Bibliographies may be arranged by author, by subject or chronologically, and may carry annotations, abstracts or critical comments, in addition to basic bibliographical information, though these will obviously make a bibliography larger and more expensive. The most common arrangement, particularly if the bibliography is a large one, is by subject.

Although it contains faults, the most significant bibliography of books (and other separates such as pamphlets and reports) so far published is the *International computer bibliography*. This was compiled by the Studiecentrum voor Informatica and published in 1968 jointly by the Studiecentrum and the National Computing Centre (UK). The work contains entries for more than 6,000 items, mostly held in the library of the Studiecentrum. The bibliography is arranged by a revised edition of the Studiecentrum classification scheme, and there are author and subject indexes. The annotations are English, German or French and the works cited are drawn from the USA and East and West Europe. A supplementary volume appeared in 1971 containing an additional 1,200 items published up to mid-1970. The supplement contains, as well as the usual author and subject indexes, additional indexes of bibliographies, standards, statistical material and dictionaries. The faults in this work are mainly the consequence of inproportionate consideration of the holdings of the Studiecentrum library. Not enough effort has been made to use the US and UK national bibliographies to ensure comprehensive coverage of English language books. On the other hand, it is strong in other European languages and in general interest trade literature. In all, however, the most useful bibliography that a librarian can hope to have on his shelves.

Another large bibliography is the *Computer literature bibliography* 2 volumes (National Bureau of Standards, 1965 and 1968). Both volumes of this work were compiled by W W Youden. This is a KWIC index of items which have appeared in nine journals, more than 100 sets of conference proceedings and twenty one books (Volume 1), and seventeen journals, twenty books and forty three conference proceedings (Volume 2). It is arranged in three sections: the ' Bibliography section ' arranges items by title abbreviation (coden), then date, issue number and initial page number (giving title and authors). The ' Title word index ' is a KWIC index to the titles referring back to the coden. The 'Author index ' gives authors' names, as much of the titles as possible, and the coden. This is an impressive bibliography in terms of number of references (6,100 in the first volume and 5,200 in the second volume), but the KWIC listing makes the bibliography very difficult to use in practice. It covers the period 1946-1967.

As well as the *International computer bibliography,* the library of the Studiecentrum voor Informatica has always issued bibliographies. Some more recent ones have been available from a commercial publisher as *Involvement of computers in medical sciences* (1,300 abstracts with author and subject indexes), *Computers and education* (over 1,800 abstracts), *Audiovisual media for computer education* (a catalog of over 400 films), *Data banks* (249 abstracts).

Some other recent bibliographies include M Gotterer *KWIC index to computer management* (Auerbach), which contains over 5,000 entries—unusually the bibliography section is annotated; the second volume of *Computer yearbook and directory*

(1969), containing an index of periodical articles and books from 1962-1968 under alphabetical subject headings, the third volume (1969) covering R and D reports under seven broad headings, with author and organisation indexes; *Bibliography on the application of computers in the construction industry 1962-1967*, published by HMSO for the Ministry of Public Building and Works in 1968 and updated every six months; and *Computing reviews*, which regularly publishes good bibliographies.

This chapter can only highlight a few of the major general bibliographies, but it may be of interest at this stage to list some other guides to the computing literature and to other areas which include computing. All of these are of some interest, and look at computer information in different ways from the present book.

Carter, C M: *Guide to reference sources in the computer sciences*. CCM Information Corporation. Announced for 1972.

Hoffmann, W: *Computer literature survey, an annotated bibliography* (translated from two issues of *Blätter der Deutschen gesellschaft für versicherungsmathematik* and probably is a precursor of the next item). IBM Research Center, Yorktown Heights, 1958. 42p.

Hoffmann, W: *Entwicklungsbericht und literaturzusammenstellung über ziffernrechenautomaten* in W Hoffman (editor): *Digitale informationswandler*. Vieweg, Braunshweig, 1962, 650-717.

McGee, W C: ' Role of the literature.' *Data processing digest,* March 1967, 1-34.

Moore, C K and Spencer, K J: *Electronics: a bibliographical guide*. Macdonald 1961, 1965, two volumes.

Morrill, C: *Computers and data processing information sources*. Gale Research, 1969.

Morrill, C: *Systems and procedures including office management information sources*. Gale Research, 1967.

Quinn, K T: 'A brief bibliographic guide to information sources on computers.' *Scientific information notes,* November-December 1969, 290-297.

Quinn, K T: *Guide to literature on computers.* American Society for Engineering Information, 1970. 10p.

The most useful guide to bibliographies in computing is the volume on *Computers and control* which is being prepared for the publishers Macdonald in their ' Bibliographic guide ' series. This will be a comprehensive guide to the most significant papers, reviews, bibliographies and reference books in these two fields.

CONTROL OF BIBLIOGRAPHIES

The bibliographies noted in this chapter are only a small selection of those available. Other bibliographies can be traced in a number of ways.

For the main computer bibliographies the abstracting journals are the most useful. Most abstracting journals either have sections in which bibliographies or references to them are collected in one place, or an index. *Computer and information systems* and *Computing reviews* adopt the former policy, while *Computer abstracts* and *Computer and control abstracts* the latter. In CCA, bibliographies have a special index in each monthly and six-monthly index, and the number of references is given.

Another useful source is *Bibliographic index* (1937-), publshed quarterly by the H W Wlson Co, who are responsible for a large number of indexing services. This particular one collects together all bibliographies appearing in the several thousand periodicals indexed by the company and in all books listed in their *Cumulative book index.* It is arranged by alphabetical subject headings, and cumulates annually and approximately three-yearly.

The National Reference Library for Science and Invention in London maintains a card index of bibliographies, which includes separately published works, those appearing as parts of other works, and abstracting and indexing services. Within the subject headings (' electronic calculating machines ' for computers) entries are arranged by date.

127

Bibliographies appearing as reports will be abstracted in *Government reports announcements*. In addition, the Special Libraries Association journal *Sci-tech news* is particularly good for these.

18 GLOSSARIES AND DICTIONARIES

IN ANY RELATIVELY new subject of study, work at first proceeds without thought of the language involved. The result of this is that after a time a point of confusion is reached when different terminology is discovered to be used for identical processes, operations and equipment, and, conversely, the same words are used for different processes, etc.

At this stage the need is therefore realised, and met, for some form of word list which can define and explain the special words in use. This is also necessary so that non specialists can understand computer terms that are in use.

In this chapter, word lists are divided into two classes: ' glossaries ' are monolingual works which define terms—their titles may include the words ' glossary ', ' dictionary ' or ' encyclopedia '; ' dictionary ', on the other hand, is applied to those works which translate languages—they usually do not define terms.

GLOSSARIES

There are three truly authoritative glossaries, which will eventually be superseded by an ISO glossary.

The earliest work is BS 3527: 1962 ' *Glossary of terms used in automatic data processing* (British Standards Institution), which defines about 700 terms, arranged in a classified order, recommending which should be used. There are tables, figures and an alphabetic index.

The *IFIP-ICC vocabulary of information processing* (North-Holland, 1966) includes about 1,200 terms, again in a classified order, defining and recommending usage. Each classified sec-

129

tion is preceded by a synoptic layout which indicates relationships between terms. Within the main groups each term is given a number, as this work is intended to be a series of glossaries which can then be used as a dictionary by cross referencing on the term number. The German language glossary has appeared as *IFIP fachwörterbuch der informationsverarbeitung* (North-Holland, 1968).

A very similar work to the *IFIP vocabulary* is the *IFIP guide to concepts and terms in data processing* (edited by I Gould, North-Holland, 1971). It can be considered a new and revised edition of the earlier work, and is similarly organised into sixteen sections, within which terms are defined. There is an alphabetical index of both preferred and non-preferred terms. It is in two volumes: the first the main English language text, and the second a multilingual vocabulary containing key-ordered and alphabetical word lists in various languages.

Finally, there is the *American national standard vocabulary for information processing* (ANSI, 1970), which was first published in 1966 and has also been reprinted by at least Honeywell and IBM. This is an alphabetic list of terms and includes a useful bibliography of other glossaries in computers and related fields.

ISO is, at present, undertaking work on a glossary which is heavily based upon those of IFIP, BSI and ANSI. It is being used also as a basis for an update of BS3527.

One general criticism that can be made of all these standards is that there is too heavy an emphasis on computing science and technology and too few definitions of terms in such areas as data processing management.

There are many commercially published glossaries of data processing and related fields. A British one is *A dictionary of computers*, edited by A Chandor (Penguin, 1970), which includes about 3,000 terms. The normal definitions are interspersed with seventy general articles on computer and business topics, which are listed at the beginning of the book and also include literature references. This is a particularly valuable glossary which includes much commercial and management material as well as computing science terms.

The more important US glossaries are:

Composition Information Services. *Glossary of automated typesetting and related computer terms.* 2nd edition, 1966.

Holmes, J F: *Data transmission and data processing dictionary.* Rider, 1965.

Horn, J: *Computer and data processing dictionary and guide.* Prentice-Hall, 1966. Includes appendices on languages, flowcharts, organisations, data representation and number systems, as well as bibliographies of books and other glossaries.

IBM have published many different glossaries, details of which are best obtained from the company or from bibliographies.

Jordain, P B: *Condensed computer encyclopedia.* McGraw-Hill, 1969. This consists of somewhat longer articles, together with an alphabetical index and a bibliography of books. The index data is computer generated and a FORTRAN program listing for this is included.

Meeks glossary of computer terminology (CCM Information) will include multiple definitions from different sources.

Polon, D D: *DCCSA dictionary of computer and control systems abbreviations signs and symbols.* Odyssey Press, 1965. This book contains information on all types of symbols, both graphic and letter, and on abbreviations of government departments and societies.

Prentice-Hall: *Encyclopedic dictionary of systems and procedures.* 1966.

Rodgers, H A: *Funk and Wagnalls dictionary of data processing terms.* 1970. Includes appendices on flowcharting and coded character sets.

Sippl, C J: *Computer dictionary and handbook.* Foulsham-Sams, 1966. Includes more than 5,000 terms, with many appendices on general topics such as equipment, programming languages, management techniques, etc. Some of the appendices are specialist glossaries, *eg* on acronyms, mathematics and statistics.

Spencer, D D: *Computer programmers' dictionary and handbook.* Blaisdell, 1968. About 1,200 terms plus appendices.

Other glossaries appear as part of more general works, such

131

as *Computer yearbook and directory* and *Computer industry annual*. To be published in the UK by Business Books is a volume on data processing in the series International dictionaries of science and technology. The English language section defines terms.

In Europe, glossaries are published by standards bodies such as DIN and AFNOR. There are also books such as:

Löbel, G: *Lexikon der datenverarbeitung*. Verlag Moderne Industrie, 1969. This contains about 3,000 terms and is illustrated by figures and photographs.

Schneider, C: *Datenverarbeitungs-lexikon*. Verlag Gabler. This also includes about 3,000 terms, with an English to German dictionary and information on machine characteristics, flowchart symbols, organisations and a chronology.

DICTIONARIES

As well as the IFIP *Vocabulary* and *Guide to concepts and terms,* the planned Business Books volume and the book by Schneider mentioned in the previous section, the following major translating dictionaries are available:

Bürger, E: *Four-language technical dictionary of data processing computers and office machinery*. Pergamon, 1970. This contains 13,000 terms in English, German, French and Russian. It is in four sections, with each language brought to the front in turn.

Camille, C and Dehaine, M: *Dictionary of data processing*. Harrap, 1970, two volumes. This is an English to French and French to English translating dictionary.

Clason, W E: *Elsevier's dictionary of automation, computers, control and measuring in six languages*. Elsevier, 1961. 3,390 terms are arranged by the English term, with indexes for Dutch, French, German, Italian and Spanish. There is a bibliography of glossaries and textbooks. A Russian supplement was published in 1962. A new edition is

Clason, W E: *Elsevier's dictionary of computers, automatic control and data processing*. Elsevier, 1971. This now includes 3,996 terms in the six languages.

132

Ginguay, M: *Dictionnaire d'informatique.* Masson, Paris, second edition, 1971. An English to French dictionary.

Hofmann, E: *Wörterbuch datenverarbeitung: Englisch-Deutsch, Deutsch-Englisch.* Berlin, Verlag die Wirtschaft, third edition, 1971.

Holland, W B: *Russian-English dictionary of cybernetics and computer technology.* Rand Corporation, second edition, 1969. (RM-5108).

Kotz, S: *Russian-English dictionary and reader in the cybernetical sciences.* Academic Press, 1966.

Kruger, K-H: *Data processing dictionary.* Verlag Dokumentation, 1968. An English to German translating dictionary which contains a useful bibliography of other glossaries and dictionaries.

Schloms, I: *Fachwörterbuch für programmierer: dictionary of programming terms.* Alfred Huthig Verlag, 1966. About 2,500 terms in French, English and German.

Trollhaun, C and Wittmann, A: *Elsevier's dictionary of data processing.* Elsevier, 1964. This includes about 4,500 terms and phrases in English, followed by their French and German equivalents, with indexes in French and German. A new edition has been published by North-Holland.

CONTROL OF GLOSSARIES AND DICTIONARIES

1 All normal book sources apply to these forms. Abstracting journals are also useful both for books and glossaries published as periodical articles.

2 The National Reference Library for Science and Invention maintains a card index of glossaries and dictionaries (including those in other books) in two sequences: by language and by subject.

3 *Bibliography of interlingual scientific and technical dictionaries* (UNESCO, fifth edition, 1969). This arranges over 2,500 dictionaries by UDC, with a key to languages translated into and from. There are indexes of languages, authors and subjects.

19 STANDARDS

'STANDARDS ARE documents formulated by agreement, authority or custom of sponsors, to define a product, material, process or procedure, quality, construction, operating characteristics, performance nomenclature and other like facts'—A S Tayal, 'Standard specifications in libraries' *Unesco bulletin for libraries* 15 (4) July-August 1961, 203-205.

An excellent overview of standards work in the computer field, which is still valid, was published in volume 8 of *Advances in computers* (Academic Press, 1967, 103-152), 'Standards for computers and information processing' by J B Steel. In addition, articles appear frequently in the professional press on various more specific aspects of standardisation.

Standards producing bodies may be manufacturers, government agencies, professional or trade associations, international organisations or the official standards body of the country.

Manufacturers produce standards primarily for their own use and for suppliers of equipment or components. Inevitably, however, the practices common among the leading manufacturers in a technology must greatly influence any later official discussions on new standards. In particular, IBM has had a tremendous influence on programming languages (FORTRAN and PL/1) and other standards. They also publish internally many which are 'computer' standards, as well as others for such products as the paint to be used on the metalwork of machines. Manufacturers' standards are rarely listed in any formal manner, except the IBM ones, which appear in their monthly publication *IBM documents*. One area in which manufacturers and software houses have issued a number of standards is data processing management, where organisations such as Hoskyns, Brandon, ICL, NCC, Honeywell, etc have issued guidelines and standards for systems and program documentation and for project control.

Government departments and agencies produce standards which, especially in the USA because of the very large government market, have a considerable impact on the computing community generally. This arises primarily from the need to lay down standards for suppliers of equipment and components. This type of standard is best illustrated by that range known as ' MIL specs ', some of which cover computers and peripherals, and these are indexed in the general *Index of federal specifications and standards* and in *Index of specifications and standards* (Department of Defence).

Of considerably more interest, however, are the series published by the National Bureau of Standards as FIPS Publications (Federal information processing standards publications). The NBS has responsibility within the federal government for monitoring and co-ordinating the development of standards as prescribed by PL 89-306 and a Bureau of the budget circular. The standards are divided into four areas: general, hardware (codes and media), software (documentation) and data (representations and codes). The annual index lists FIPS PUBS, articles appearing in the FIPS Notes column of the *NBS technical news bulletin,* publishes federal policy and procedural guideline documents (including PL 89-306) and outlines federal, ANSI and ISO standardisation activities.

Some of the FIPS standards represent the adoption of existing standards, but others are generated within the government itself (*eg* the codes for metropolitan statistical areas).

In the UK the major semi-governmental agency involved in publishing standards is the NCC, which has issued the systems documentation standards and is working on standards in other areas of data processing management.

Professional bodies in the UK do not usually issue standards on their own account. Most of their work is done through representation on the relevant BSI committee. In the field of professional ethics, however, BCS has published a ' Code of conduct ' and a ' Code of good practice ', and codes of practice also have been adopted by both the Computer Service Bureau Association and the Software Houses Association.

In the US, on the other hand, more than one-third of the standards published by ANSI were first developed by professional or trade organisations. In addition, the IEEE, as well as its standards on components such as semiconductors, has published a number of standards on information processing, including two glossaries. The ACM regularly publishes in the *Communications of the ACM* new and proposed ANSI standards, together with comments on them. The Data Processing Management Association does the same in *Data management*.

International organisations which are involved with computers are only three in number. The International Organisation for Standardisation (ISO) has as members the national standards body of each country. Standards are developed by technical committees, of which TC 97 covers computers and information processing. TC 97 is subdivided into eight subcommittees, most of which have working groups. In the past, approved standards have been issued as ISO recommendations, which are then generally adopted by national bodies. From 1972, however, ISO will publish Standards. Recommendations and Standards are listed in the *ISO memento*. The International Electrotechnical Commission has a technical committee working on data processing standards, and co-operates closely with ISO. The European Computer Manufacturers Association has issued over twenty standards (the majority compatible with ISO documents), together with some other material, *eg COBOL translations*.

The national bodies of the UK and US have already been mentioned, and it is they who produce the most significant standards in computing. ANSI (previously ASA and USASI) operates technically in the following manner. Beneath the administrative structure are a number of standards boards, each responsible for several efforts in a particular area of a standardisation. One board is the Information Processing Systems Standards Board, which has reporting to it standards committees on computers and information processing, office machines, vocabulary for automatic control, and library sciences and documentation.

Each Committee is sponsored by a trade or professional association—the Business Equipment Manufacturers Association in the case of x3 (computers and information processing), and membership is open to organisations. x3 then controls three groups (hardware, software and systems) which, in turn, have a total of eight sections (recognition, physical media, data representation, documentation, language, data communications, system technology, and system measurements). At this level and beneath, members serve as technically qualified individuals. Each section in turn divides into Working Groups, eg language into FORTRAN, COBOL, ALGOL and APT.

A complete list of ANSI standards is available in the annual *Catalog of standards,* but the following should be noted: the *Vocabulary for information processing* (revised 1970), the code for information interchange and the language codes—especially FORTRAN.

BSI is, in broad outline, similarly organised, although membership of technical committees is on an organisational rather than a personal basis. Technically, the Data Processing Industry committee forms part of the Engineering Division. Beneath the main committee are about twenty technical committees, where the main work of standards production is done. These committees cover such topics as punched cards, keyboards, character recognition, safety, etc. One standard which does not originate from this committee is BS 1000A (681.3), which is the computer schedule for UDC.

British standards are listed with abstracts and an index in the annual *British standards yearbook.* During the year, new, revised and withdrawn standards appear in the monthly *BSI news.* A very useful supplement to the *Yearbook* is *Publications by international organisations,* which includes ISO and IEC standards. There is a UDC index which also includes British standards.

The ANSI annual *Catalog of standards* lists titles only arranged by the main committees, together with a subject index and a cross index between ANSI numbers and the reference numbers allotted by other organisations (*eg* IEEE) whose standards have been endorsed by ANSI. It includes, also, international standards, and has a useful list of official standards bodies in other countries.

The standards bodies in other countries operate in a similar manner. Two of the most important ones are the Association Française de Normalisation (AFNOR) and the Deutsche Normenausschuss (which issues standards with the DIN prefix). Both publish annual catalogs. Many Russian standards on computing (from their standards organisation GOST) are published as AD reports, being translated by Foreign Technology Division (USAF).

20 DIRECTORIES AND COMPANY DATA

TRADE DIRECTORIES are used to trace the manufacturer of a particular product or a company that offers a particular service. They may well include much other information, and a glance at some of the descriptions below will show just how wide in scope this additional information can be. Their primary function, however, is to give company information. This information can vary from just the name, address, telephone and telex numbers, to a considerable amount of detail on the key personnel in the firm, its corporate structure, services and subsidiaries.

The layout of this chapter is a grouping by country, with a section at the end on international directories. It must not be forgotten that, in addition to the directories described here, the periodical and report literature frequently includes directory information.

UNITED KINGDOM

There are two main directories in the UK : *Computer directory* and *Computer users' yearbook*.

Computer directory (1970-) is published by *Computer weekly* and contains purely company information. It is divided into six sections : services—a subject guide to the activities of software houses, service bureaux, data preparation bureaux, time brokers, consultants, educational establishments, staff agencies, etc; fields of application—a subject guide to fields within which consultancy or programming companies work; mainframe, ancillary and peripheral equipment and supplies; societies—associations and institutes, etc, computer user groups, member societies of IFIP; main company section—alphabetical list by company, giving offices, personnel, languages, services, equipment, software packages, etc; combined index to the subject headings in the first three sections.

Computer users' yearbook (1969-) is a much larger and more complex work. There is a number of sections, each generally headed by a general article and followed by directory information. The sections are: recruitment services (this also includes a salary analysis); training facilities and courses, divided into eleven areas such as systems analysis, or operating; practical information on character codes; data processing standards (articles); associations, institutions and societies; equipment and supplies, including charts of equipment and peripheral characteristics; site preparation services; consultants, software houses and programming services; service bureaux; data preparation bureaux; directory of UK computer installations.

As described previously, *Computer survey* has directory information on bureaux and on computer and peripheral equipment. The Computer Consultants volume *Computers in Europe* has information on manufacturers, and their new work on *Computer peripheral equipment* also includes company information.

David Rayner Associates publish a number of company directories in the general field of electronics which are of interest. In particular, *Industrial and scientific instruments and systems* (1971) includes companies working in the field of process control systems. Another (planned) publication covers computer hardware, software and services companies.

NCC maintains a background index containing records of all companies in the UK offering computer services or services to the computer industry. Information is collected by means of questionnaires and updated regularly. Periodicals are also scanned, and information gleaned from these is added to the company files.

A specialist directory is the *BCS educational yearbook*, which, as well as containing state of the art articles, has directory information on courses, lists of films, educational equipment, etc.

Financial information on UK computer companies is best obtained from the data processing section of Extract Information Services. This is a card service which summarises the latest accounts of what will, eventually, be about 500 companies. Very few of the companies appear in the major general financial services such as Moodies.

Finally, bodies such as the Software Houses Association and COSBA issue directories of their members and members services.

Computer yearbook and directory includes directory information on manufacturers and products as well as user groups, associations, publishers, university centres and special features on insurance and bank installations.

The *Computer industry annual* includes detailed comparison charts of equipment, a product and services directory and a manufacturers' directory, which goes into more detail on each company. *Datamation industry directory* contains similar information.

Specialist directories include the *Data communications buyers' guide* published by the magazine *Telecommunications* and the *Computer education directory*. The latter includes information on books, films, courses, etc.

Published as an annual supplement to the June issue of *Computers and automation* is the *Computer directory and buyers' guide*. The sections of the 1971 edition of the directory are: roster of programming languages 1971 by Jean Sammet (a useful update to her book—see page 157); a classified list of over 2,100 applications of computers; characteristics of digital computers and list of manufacturers (taken from *Computer characteristics review*); world computer census; main roster of organisations in computers and data processing; buyers' guide to products and services; geographic roster of organisations; supplementary roster of organisations (companies who did not respond to the 1971 questionnaire); college and university computer facilities; computer associations; information on chapters of the DPMA; chapters of the ACM; ACM special interest groups and committees; computer users groups.

Another annual supplement is the September issue of *Busi-*

ness automation, which includes equipment characteristics of: data display equipment, office copiers, facsimile equipment and microfilm equipment of all types; and brief equipment descriptions of: film systems for computer input and output, automated film systems, modems and acoustic couplers, data communication terminals, key-to-tape equipment, data collection equipment, optical and mark sense scanners, electronic accounting machines. These are followed by an alphabetic listing of companies and a buyers' guide. Because of the volume of equipment available, comparison charts are separately available for many of the classes of equipment not listed above as having such charts in the actual issue.

Datapro 70 is a general looseleaf directory which attempts to include only the most significant material in its sections on computers, peripheral equipment, software packages and companies. Each report is divided into two parts—characteristics which are purely factual and management reports which give evaluative comment.

Other specialist directories include the *ADAPSO directory of data processing service centres* (annual), *Directory of computerized information in science and technology* (Science Associates/International), which lists machine-readable data bases of (mainly) technical literature, the *Time-sharing industry directory,* and *Software contractors: credentials and capabilities* (System Interaction Corporation), which is a looseleaf service reporting on software companies in some detail.

All of the hardware and software information services also include directory information.

EUROPE

There are not many directories covering individual countries. Two known ones are *Zero un scope rouge* (annual, Editions Tests), which lists French companies both alphabetically and classified under products and services; and *Branchen-index der datenverarbeitung* (Informationsbüro für Datenverarbeitung, 1971), which gives 1,500 addresses of German companies in the hardware and software fields.

Three international directories exist. The *International directory of computer and information system services 1971* (Europa Publications for the Intergovernmental Bureau for Informatics, Rome) replaces the *International repertory of computation laboratories*. It lists 2,500 organisations offering services in more than seventy countries throughout the world. Each country has its entries subdivided into national centres, education and training institutions, universities and colleges, government establishments and agencies, research institutions, consultants and service bureaux. Each entry includes details of name and address, officers, present equipment, languages, contemplated equipment, services available, application fields and training offered. There are two indexes—one of institutions and one by computer.

Computer Consultants Ltd publish annually *Who is related to whom in the computer industry,* which provides names and addresses of all manufacturers directly engaged in the industry and cross references between parent and subsidiary organisations. Indexes are to countries and fields of activity.

The world directory of computer companies (annual 1970-) is published by Computer Publications Inc (Newport Beach, California). It includes a main section listing companies alphabetically, together with a subject index to their interests, a personnel index, a listing of associations and a calendar of events. The companies covered are those in all areas of computing, *ie* hardware—mainframes, peripherals and components; software and services—leasing, education, supplies, etc.

CONTROL OF DIRECTORIES

The normal book sources such as *British national bibliography* ought to include all commercially published directories. In addition, however, there are specialist sources for tracing directories. G P Henderson has compiled *Current British directories* (CBD research), and the same company publishes *Current European directories* (1969). Both of these books reach the usual very high standards of comprehensiveness and indexing of this firm.

Equivalent American sources are *Guide to American directories* edited by B Klein (8th edition, 1971) and foreign directories by *Trade directories of the world* (Croner), an annual looseleaf publication with supplements. For current awareness *Datamation* and *FID news bulletin* are especially good.

21 HARDWARE INFORMATION SOURCES

THIS CHAPTER COVERS all those publications which list, usually in tabulated form, the characteristics of computers and associated equipment. There are very many of these publications and the selection of the right one for any particular need may not be at first sight, an easy matter. In detail, publications range from the brief information on internal characteristics, input-output and cost appearing in the directory issue of *Computers and automation* and in *Computer characteristics review* to the massive evaluative details in the *Standard EDP reports*.

Auerbach Info Inc are the major producers of reference material on hardware and (latterly) software. They are the most authoritative and in many ways, unless the simple checking of a fact (*eg* the number of index registers) is required, the most useful. Even for the simple fact, however, it will often be only Auerbach which supplies it. In spite of their size, the logical breakdown of the reports and the detailed subject indexes make information very easy to find.

Auerbach publications are organised into 4 series : Computer technology reports, Computer technology state of the arts series, Computer technology digest series, and Computer technology guide series.

The major data compilations appear in the Computer technology reports series, all others being condensations of these. Within this series the major work is the *Standard EDP reports*. These are in eleven volumes, eight covering general purpose US computers (Burroughs, CDC, General Electric, Honeywell, IBM, Monrobot, NCR, RCA, Scientific Data Systems and Univac) and three minicomputers (thirty five manufacturers). The minicomputer volumes are also available separately as *Minicomputer reports* (previously *Scientific and control computer reports*), as are the other volumes of the *Standard EDP reports*.

Each report consists of a system summary followed by a very detailed survey and associated tabular data. The reports follow a consistent logical pattern and the main headings are: data structure; system configuration; internal storage; central processor; console; input-output: printers; input-output: magnetic tape; input-output: communications; simultaneous operations; instruction list; data codes; problem orientated facilities; process orientated language; COBOL; machine orientated language; program translator; operating environment; system performance (benchmark tests); physical characteristics; price data.

Additional to the reports are a users' guide (the background to the reports, under the same headings); glossary; comparison charts; selection procedure (systems analysis); directories and special reports (state of the art reviews).

Although, at present, *Standard EDP reports* covers only US machines, it is intended progressively to include computers from Europe and Japan, starting with ICL machines. There is also the possibility that they will be reorganised and arranged by the subject matter of the reports rather than by machine. Thus, all CPUs can be directly compared.

A number of summaries of the *Standard EDP reports* are published. *Computer notebook international* (two volumes) contains the users' guide, glossary, comparison charts, special reports and the system summaries and price lists for each machine included. The machines are those of the US manufacturers listed above, plus the major manufacturers from Denmark, France, Israel, Italy, Japan, Netherlands, UK and West Germany. It is from the system summaries of the foreign machines that the full reports are being prepared, so that *Computer notebook international* will be a complete subset of the *Standard EDP reports* instead of containing some unique material. *Software notebook,* described more fully in chapter 22, essentially consists of the system summary, part of the detailed reports and price lists. *Minicomputer notebook* (one volume) consists of the summaries, comparison charts and price lists. *Computer charac-*

146

teristics digest is a quarterly bound volume which reprints the prices and comparison charts.

Other Auerbach services in the Computer technology reports series maintain the same high standard. *Data communications reports* covers communications systems design, common-carrier facilities, comparison charts and detailed reports on communications terminal equipment (including teleprinters, keyboard/display systems, magnetic and paper tape terminals, and multifunction terminals), facsimile equipment and communications processing equipment (including audio response units). A one volume summary, *Communications terminal digest,* includes the comparison charts on the equipment (250 communications and seventy five alpha-numeric display terminals) and systems design material.

Data handling reports has comparison charts and reports on desk-type and portable calculators, data transcription equipment, input preparation equipment, source data recording equipment, forms handling equipment, supplies and a directory of manufacturers.

Graphic processing reports covers graphic image processing equipment and software *eg* automatic photocomposition devices, alpha-numeric and graphic data displays, electromechanical plotters, CRT display copiers, computer output microfilmers, digitisers, microfilm information systems and video image systems. The usual comparison charts, special reports and directory appear.

Time sharing reports covers the complete field of timesharing: applications programs and libraries, languages, equipment and commercial services, as well at tutorial articles and comparison charts.

Software reports is in this series and is more fully described in chapter 22.

Computer technology digest series consists of the *Communications terminals digest* and *Computer characteristics digest.* The state of the art series consists, so far, of *Auerbach on time sharing,* primarily a discursive guide to the evaluation of systems, services, languages and equipment, but including some comparison charts. Computer technology guide series consists of the *Guide to data communications* and the *Guide to mini-computers*. Both include discursive material outlining principles and characteristics of representative systems.

All other systems duplicate Auerbach to some extent, although somewhat more cheaply. Some of the more important services are described below :

GML corporation publish two services (both previously published by Keydata) which have been in existence for a number of years. *Computer characteristics review* appears every four months and summarises price and performance data on 350 central processors, and over 1,000 peripheral devices from the US, Europe and Japan. The section on central processors gives information on processor speed, internal storage, instruction set, input-output, auxiliary storage, etc; that on peripherals covers auxiliary storage, magnetic tape, card equipment, line printers and paper tape equipment; comparative information sections cover compatibility of peripherals and processors, a listing by system configurations giving price, applications and ranked lists by internal storage characteristics.

Computer display review, now comprising four large looseleaf volumes, gives detailed reports upon alpha-numeric and graphic displays, recorders and scanners, digital-to-video converters, light pens and other display equipment. There is much discursive material outlining display fundamentals and applications, as well as a directory and a bibliography. An interesting feature is the contributed papers which appear at the end of several sections and are reprints of journal articles and research reports.

Business automation product information services (formerly *Office automation*) appears in three hardware volumes—Microfilm and copiers. Computer devices (all major manufactured computers and minicomputers plus input devices and printers) and Peripherals edition (OCR, data transmission, collection and display equipment). Comparison charts and reports are included.

The journal *Modern data* publishes a series called *Techfiles.* These are twelve looseleaf volumes with quarterly updates which present basic reviews, product comparison charts, market studies, bibliographies of manufacturers' literature and directories in such areas as interactive CRT displays, minicomputers, OCR and mark readers, plotters and COM.

Data processing systems encyclopedia has sections on: computer ' specs '; software; computers and computer systems; data collection communications and transmission systems; displays and graphics ; financial—prices and rentals ; historical ; peripheral ; punch card and special equipment.

In the United Kingdom there are only a few data compilations of this type. Computer Consultants Ltd issue several of them. *Computers in Europe* (1971) replaces *British commercial computer digest* (eleventh edition), *European computer user's handbook* (seventh edition) and *European computer survey* (sixth edition). It contains a list of and short notes on: European digital computers, electronic calculators, direct access computers, accounting and invoicing machines, analog computers, and peripheral equipment, together with a list of manufacturers. *Current computers* (two volumes : 1969, 1971) contains details of 214 computers in current use in Europe in 1969 and 178 computers announced between 1969 and late 1971. It contains descriptions and technical details of computers and peripheral equipment. *Computer peripheral equipment* (1971) brings together into one volume all peripherals and provides more technical detail. Two other older but still interesting volumes from this publisher are *A record of vintage computers,* which includes a very useful cross reference index of computer names, and *A report on computers in Russia* (1966), which includes general data on the USSR and details of peripherals, current and older digital computers, special purpose computers, analog computers, hybrid computers, calculators, computer manufacturers, and a look at the future.

NCC's hardware index contains detailed information on all hardware available in the UK together with much information on purely US material. Where possible, information is verified by means of standard questionnaires and thus equipment can be directly evaluated. Two publications giving technical data

149

have appeared based upon the hardware index—one on *Visible record computers* and the other upon *Keyboard/printer terminals.*

Other sources of hardware information include periodicals such as *Computer weekly, Datamation, Peripherals bulletin, Informatique digest,* etc, most of the general directories such as *Computer users' yearbook* and *Computer industry annual,* other information services such as the BCS library and Computer Information Centre, and special reports such as those by the Electrical Research Association and Programming Sciences International on minicomputers or C G Baker Associates on COM.

22 SOFTWARE INFORMATION SOURCES

IT IS HIGHLY significant that the first edition of this book did not include a single specialist software information source. In the intervening years, the importance of software has grown so much that there is now a large variety of means by which it can be bought, sold and exchanged. As has been previously shown, it is in software that the greatest expenditure of a computer installation is incurred. The IFIP Administration Data Processing Group has shown concern over the past years and has held many conferences on the ' not invented here ' syndrome, *ie* the unwillingness of computer users to use other people's software and their regular insistence on writing their own.

One of the reasons for this is, undoubtedly, the poor quality of packages in the past, where there was no guarantee that the package would work, little documentation, no user training, etc—not so much software as ' flabbyware '! Another is that data processing is essentially an odd mixture of a craft, an art and engineering. Practical on-the-job work is more highly prized than careful searching to eliminate duplication, such as is carried out much more frequently in a scientific discipline such as chemistry.

A start has been made to break through this barrier by the Software Verification Service of NCC. In this service each item of software is entered onto the National Computer Program Index by means of a questionnaire. Each supplier is therefore constrained to supply full information necessary for the evaluation of a package by a prospective purchaser. SVS proceeds in stages : in stage one, basic information is given on supplier, purpose, language and details of actual installations on which the program or package has run. Stage two goes into much more depth and attempts to utilise existing standards where possible, *eg* documentation standards, and language standards. It is not enough to know that documentation is provided—this could be notes on the back of an envelope or a two foot high stack of documents. It is important for a prospective purchaser to know which; and if a standard exists then what is supplied can be measured against this. All program interchange is aided by standards. This is most obvious with regard to programming language standards such as ANSI FORTRAN. Later stages of verification will cover the methodology of the application, *eg* does it meet the needs of the modern accountant or is it the latest and best vehicle scheduling algorithm, and the efficiency of translating this into a computer program.

This approach has obvious advantages to both supplier and prospective user. Information given to users may range from ' gossip ' to ' gospel ', *ie* from little more than a contact to fully verified to Stage *n*. The user, however, knows that verified information is good information which meets standards, and therefore the program is more likely to work. The supplier wants his information to pass through the verification process because he knows that verified information will be the first to be examined and followed up. There must always, in any information service, be room for information which may not be up to the standards of quality and completeness that one would like. Too many information services contain only incomplete information, however. The principles of svs are equally applicable to information collected by libraries and information services in other fields.

The remainder of the chapter describes sources of information on programs and software. First of all, a listing is given of the major sources of program information generally. Not all of these are described in detail later on, but they are listed here for completeness.

a) Specialist directories and abstracting services, *eg ICP quarterly*. Sometimes these may be restricted by subject or source.

152

b) Information centres. As with translation centres, these may be just indexes of programs (*eg* NCC) or may be program libraries. Program libraries are generally organised on a subject basis, often at universities, *eg* Queen's University Belfast, Indiana University (quantum chemistry).

c) Manufacturers' catalogs. Most manufacturers issue catalogs of the packages they make available—either on a bundled or unbundled basis. In some cases these are particularly comprehensive and well indexed, *eg* IBM.

d) User groups. The user groups are well known and are organised on the basis of one or more machines of an individual manufacturer's range. Many of these, such as SHARE, CO-OP and DECUS, maintain indexes, program libraries and issue catalogs of available material.

e) Subject orientated groups. Many associations or large organisations maintain indexes and libraries of programs, *eg* Heating and Ventilating Research Association, IEE, American Bankers Association, government departments such as Department of the Environment, and Civil Service Department, and bodies such as Euratom and USAEC. The nuclear field is particularly well organised, with a complex network of libraries and interchange agreements between governments, universities and industry in Europe, UK, USA and Canada.

f) The literature. Computing literature abounds with descriptions of programs, as well as many actual program listings. These may appear as formal papers, in which cases they can be fairly easily picked up through abstracting journals. Many, however, are but brief descriptions from press releases to new magazines or appear in ' software available ' columns in periodicals.

UNITED KINGDOM

The major source of program information in the UK is, of course, the NCC, which has as one of its indexes the National Computer Program Index. NCPI contains about 8,000 abstracts of programs available in the United Kingdom. As described

153

above, the usefulness of this index has been enhanced by the introduction of the Software Verification Service.

Most of the programs are held in the computer based information retrieval system and are indexed using the *NCC thesaurus of computing terms.* The NCPI contains a fair range of programs across many areas of science, technology and commerce. In addition, an effort is made to collect other software catalogs so that a comprehensive service can be offered.

An additional index at NCC is PROSSIR (Program Software and System name Index-Register) which contains records of named programs.

The other major service is *Co-pac index,* a looseleaf collection of program abstracts arranged in three main areas (system and peripheral software, business applications, and technical and scientific applications), each further subdivided. A keyword index is provided and there are lists of contributors and their services. Later updates have included sections on training courses and computer time for sale. The disadvantage of the *Co-pac index* is that only the briefest details are given about the purpose and implementation of the program. To receive further information (including the name of the supplier) a fee must be paid. This contrasts with NCPI, where full information is given in the program abstract but nothing is provided for browsing.

Other specialist directories in the UK include the annual *Computers in the environmental sciences,* edited by J R Tarrant (published by the University of East Anglia). The 1971 edition contained 250 program abstracts—mostly UK but with some foreign and US ones. The Heating and Ventilating Research Association have published a list of UK programs in the heating, ventilating and air conditioning fields as part of an international exercise.

One other potentially valuable source is *Software world.* This quarterly journal, as well as carrying normal articles, has extensive lists of available programs and literature on programs. These are also carried in *Software monthly.* Unfortunately, this journal is not indexed, and consequently what must be at least 500 programs a year remain buried somewhere in its pages, unless indexed individually by many recipient libraries which is very wasteful.

UNITED STATES

As always, the United States has a wealth of program sources, with many co-operative program libraries and well organised user groups. There are now so many of these that it is desirable that a full directory should be published, and it is to be hoped that someone in the USA will soon undertake the work.

The earliest of all sources is *Collected algorithms from CACM* (1960-), which collects into one looseleaf volume all algorithms, comments and certifications published in the 'Algorithms' column in *Communications of the ACM*. It is updated monthly and includes primarily mathematical algorithms (analysis, calculus, etc) written in Algol. There are, however, a few algorithms in other languages (Fortran and PL/1) and on other topics (sorting, plotting, etc). There is a subject index which also includes algorithms from *Computer journal, Numerische mathematik, BIT,* etc. This index is arranged by means of a classification which has been developed from an original one of SHARE. It has also been translated into Russian.

One of the oldest program package sources, which also includes some UK and European material, is *ICP quarterly* (1967-). This contains program abstracts, with information on implementation and (usually) source grouped into broad subject areas such as printing industry, banking, etc. There is an index by machine type but none by general subject. Included also are a list of time sharing services and often a general article on, *eg,* package evaluation or protection. As well as commercially available programs, COSMIC programs are included.

COSMIC is the Computer Software Management Information Centre established at the University of Georgia by NASA. It distributes to industry more generally programs which have been produced by or for NASA, DOD and USAEC, and which are considered to have potential usefulness in the private sector.

155

These programs are generally made available very cheaply. As well as appearing in *ICP quarterly*, COSMIC programs also appear in *Computer program abstracts* (1969-), a quarterly abstracting journal produced by NASA and following the STAR format almost exactly, *ie* abstracts appear in the thirty four broad subject categories and are indexed by subject, personal and corporate authors, accession and report numbers.

A more recent quarterly abstracting service is *Computer programs in science and technology* (1971-), which is somewhat more restricted in subject matter, as indicated by its title, but does include many UK programs (supplied by NCPI) and some European ones. Program information is much the same as the other services, indexes are of the supplier and keywords/subject/acronym or name. There is also a bibliography of literature describing computer programs.

There is a number of other looseleaf services which cover programs and software. These are generally updated monthly. *Business automation product information services software edition* (formerly *Business software information service*) contains full page abstracts arranged by machine, with supplier and subject indexes. There are also very useful comparative reports on particular topics such as payroll, data base management systems, etc, and a list of companies in the US who supply software.

Datapro 70 has a section on the major software packages. Each report is about two pages in length and consists of a management summary (interpretive comment by the compilers) and characteristics (a factual account of the product). Feature reports, *eg* on buying software packages, are also included.

Auerbach have also moved into the software field with the *Auerbach software reports* (1970-) and *Auerbach software notebook*. *Auerbach software reports* contain details primarily of applications packages. The packages are grouped into subject areas (*eg* production planning and control, data management, general ledger), which are preceded by general reports on the software industry and software facilities. Each application area consists of a general introduction to the application in

156

question, lengthy reports on individual packages and comparison charts which summarise the characteristics of these packages and others not described in detail.

Auerbach software notebook is extracted from the *Standard EDP reports*. It covers operating systems, compilers, assemblers, utility routines and languages of the computers included (*ie* roughly the last section of the full report), and contains less detailed information on the hardware (the first two thirds of the full report).

Other Auerbach services, such as the *Minicomputer reports* and *Time sharing reports,* also include information on relevant software.

Another looseleaf service is *Software packages: an encyclopedic guide* (1970-)—a three volume manual giving the usual factual and evaluative material. There are application, vendor, package name and hardware indexes.

Current awareness of new packages can be obtained from very many sources. Nearly all computer journals have ' New products' columns, the following being particularly good: *Software age, Software digest, Software central, Business automation, Datamation* and *Data processing magazine.*

Finally, there are many specialist and book publications on software. The most significant is *Computer programs directory* (CCM Information Corporation, 1971), which contains abstracts of more than 1,200 programs available from sixteen user groups. It is sponsored by the ACM and the Joint User Group (JUG). There is a subject index and it is intended to produce annual editions. Other software guides include *Decision table software—a handbook,* edited by H McDaniel (Auerbach Publishers, 1970), *CAI guide* (Entelek, 1968), *Index to computer aided instruction,* second edition edited by H A Lekan (Stirling Institute, 1970) and many others published as US government research reports. A most important book by Jean E Sammet, entitled *Programming languages : history and fundamentals* (Prentice Hall, 1969), is a basic reference work which describes and gives references for all major and most minor high level languages developed in the US. For many languages, sample programs are given.

There are few specialist information sources covering European programs on a commercial basis, although organisations such as the European Nuclear Energy Agency (ENEA), Euratom and COMSIS have their own specialist directories.

The only commercial service so far available is the looseleaf *European software catalog*. There is a French edition distributed by Editions Tests; with some 300 packages listed it is updated monthly. Other national editions will presumably follow.

Two North-Holland journals *Computer physics communications* and *Computer programs in biomedicine* have attempted to organise the programs reported by them. The editor of the former has set up a program library at Queen's University Belfast, while the editor of the latter has an index to programs at Uppsala University (Sweden).

158

23 INSTALLATIONS AND INDUSTRY STATISTICS

A FREQUENT ENQUIRY made of a computer information service is for installation data. This may be couched in various forms, *eg* ' Which machine has XYZ Ltd got ', 'A list of all IBM 360 series machines owned by banks in Scotland ', ' Statistics on market share of companies A, B, and C in 1960 and 1970 ', or ' How many computers will be installed in the UK in 1980?'

Thus it can be seen that an accurate register of all installations within a country (with as much detail as possible about each) is essential for purposes of marketing, sales campaigns, market research, company evaluations, crystal ball gazing, arranging back-up facilities, etc. For the purposes of general market research and estimates of trends within the computer industry, global statistics drawn from such a register are used in estimating not only such obvious areas as the growth of computers in a country over the next 10 years, but also in planning the national pattern of education in computing. From a properly drawn sample we can determine the staffing structure of installations in terms of data processing managers, systems analysts, programmers, operators and data preparation staff. The installation register will then indicate the national requirements now and in the future. It can then be determined whether the output of trained staff in the various areas will meet these requirements.

For the major countries of the world, installation registers and the statistics drawn from them are fairly readily available. In some cases, however, they may well be buried more or less helpfully in the literature. For example, *EDP europa report* regularly has features on individual European countries which give statistics in great detail. However, this magazine is not abstracted by any of the major computer abstracting services, and thus this invaluable information remains unavailable to the majority of users.

Another difficulty in using statistics of this nature is that there are considerable discrepancies, even over data relating to past installations—let alone future predictions. This is the common problem of definition. One organisation may include visible record and dedicated (process control) computers in its statistics —another may not. This can lead to variations as large as ten per cent nationally, and even greater for individual manufacturers.

The remainder of this chapter is divided into geographic areas—international, UK, US, Europe and other countries. Within each area we look at two types of data :
a) complete registers which actually list installations by company name (installation registers) and b) general industry statistics. The latter are primarily based upon installation data and sorted by manufacturer, model, sector of industry, etc. Other economic statistics are also included here, however, such as imports and exports, personnel, etc.

INTERNATIONAL

Registers : There is only one truly international register of computer installations and this is operated by a US company, International Data Corporation. The computer-based file contains information on more than 50,000 US installations and 30,000 installations throughout the rest of the world. Information held about each installation includes material on the site (company name and address, sales volume, employees, SIC codes, etc), the mainframe (core size, model, method of acquisition, etc), peripherals (card readers/punches, data collection, display or communications equipment, MICR/OCR, etc) and software (applications, operating system, programming languages).

A wide variety of statistical and full information runs can be made on this data, either on an SDI or special search basis. Since so many characteristics are included, it is possible to obtain on printout labels or tab cards very specific enquiries. The standard subfiles cover mainly geographical areas, which

160

can also be subdivided by some configuration characteristics (*eg* IBM or magnetic-tape storage). Statistics from the file are extensively used by IDC and other organisations.

Computer Consultants Ltd publish, in *Facts and figures about computers in Europe* (1971), and previously in *European computer survey*, a list of installations in sixteen European countries. Detailed statistical surveys are also included which relate to installations, industrial sector penetration, values of installations and orders, etc.

Statistics: IDC publish in *EDP industry report* and *EDP europa report* regular censuses and market analyses of the world as a whole, individual countries, classes of equipment, manufacturers, etc. *EDP industry report* produces world censuses of manufacturer and machine for general purpose and for dedicated application digital computers, which appears in alternate issues. Annual ' review and forecast ' issues interpret the statistics. *Computers and automation* produces in each issue a very similar census and also includes a regular column of new installations.

Some older statistics which are still useful cover the various European countries individually and also include information on manufacturers' market penetration. *Computers in Europe— 1966*, by W K deBruijn (NAIPRC, 1966), also includes information on personnel and penetration of computers into various sectors of industry. *Gaps in technology—electronic computers* (OECD, 1970) contains many other statistics on aspects of the industry in Europe and the USA, as well as much valuable historical material.

One other census source is ADP *newsletter*, which includes the major European countries and the USA in twice-yearly statistical issues.

UNITED KINGDOM
As well as the IDC file which covers the UK, there is one other magnetic tape service. This is operated by NCC for Pedder Associates, who supply all the input data and corrections. The contents of the file include information on the site, CPU, peri-

161

pherals, personnel, languages and software, and applications. The current installations are included in *Computer survey,* together with statistical summaries. Information on all past and present UK installations is held. The detailed information on magnetic tape will be a useful adjunct to the cheaper but less informative *Computer survey.*

The other source of UK statistics is published quarterly by the Department of Trade and Industry as the *UK computer market.* It includes primarily financial data on exports, imports and home installations for various areas of hardware, software, R&D and personnel. It is the most frequently used economic indicator for the industry. As well as the current quarter's statistics, comparative statistics are given back to 1966.

Statistical data on the UK computer industry is frequently published in the journals and as special studies. Particularly useful sources are NCC and the hearings of the Parliamentary Committee on Science and Technology (Subcommittees A and D).

UNITED STATES

In addition to IDC, there is also one other magnetic tape service of US installations which is maintained by the Computer Intelligence Corporation (San Diego). It includes information on mainframe and configuration and also statistical information on the company.

There seem to be no general printed directories of US installations.

Statistics are included in such journals as *Datamation, EDP industry report, ADP newsletter,* etc, and in the many (usually high priced) special market surveys.

EUROPE

Registers: *Zero un scope rouge* (Editions Tests, annual) is primarily a register of French installations and a detailed statistical survey. It also includes directory information. The installation data is in four main sections: alphabetically by company; geographically by department; by machine; by industrial sector. The first two sections and the last give the name of the company, the town, machine, a series of codes which indicate peripheral equipment, languages and methods of use (real time, visual display, batch processing, etc) and a brief indication of applications. The second section gives only company name and locality.

Facts and figures about computers in Europe and IDC include data on European installations.

Statistics. Statistics on European countries are regularly produced by such magazines as *EDP europa report* and the national computer journals—particularly those listed in the chapters on commercial periodicals and news periodicals. The sources described above in the international section also regularly cover Europe.

OTHER COUNTRIES

The Canadian Information Processing Society produces an annual census of Canadian installations and an annual salary/manpower survey (in October and April respectively).

Good statistics on the Japanese industry are published in the *JIPDEC report.*

24 BIOGRAPHICAL DATA

A COMMON ENQUIRY in libraries and information centres concerns individuals working in the computer field—their qualifications, publications, current employment, and so on. There are relatively few publications which help to provide this type of information, however.

Who's who in computers and data processing has been published fairly regularly for several years. The fifth edition was published in 1971 by *Computers and automation*. It contains entries for over 15,000 computer personnel in three volumes: systems analysts and programmers, data processing managers and directors, other computer professionals. Entries cover name, address, organisation, job title, education, publications, honours, membership of societies, etc. Regular amendments and new entries are published in *Computers and automation*.

There is no comparable work in the UK. To find information on individuals in this country one must go to general directories such as the *Directory of British scientists,* which lists 8,000 scientists.

A similar multi-volume work devoted to American scientists is *American men of science,* which contains more than 100,000 names, but little information about publications.

Most computer journals give some sort of information about their contributors—at the minimum his affiliation, but often a short biography, sometimes with a photograph. Assuming, therefore, that the person in whom one is interested has written a paper, in view of the high mobility of labour in the computer industry journals are likely to be more up to date than biographical directories.

A few books have been published on individual men—mostly the older figures such as Babbage and Hollerith, *eg* M Moseley *Irascible genius; a life of Charles Babbage, inventor* (Hutchinson, 1964), and of course the writings of key workers such as Babbage, Hollerith, John von Neumann, Diebold and others are generally available.

25 LIBRARIES AND ORGANISATIONS

LIKE THE ENERGY of the universe, information tends to become dispersed in time to a dead level of unavailability. It inevitably separates out into small compartments in men's minds, in their offices, in journals and in other media. Libraries seek to act in the reverse direction and to halt this process of entropy. They try to stem the dispersal of knowledge, and instead collate it, and make it or its records available together in one place.

This chapter looks briefly at some of the major computer libraries and information centres. In the section on control there are also listed some guides to general directories of research organisations, since the computer librarian very frequently requires this type of information to trace specialist bodies.

UNITED KINGDOM

The major computer libraries in the UK belong to the manufacturers, although there are a number of other organisations which have libraries in this field.

In addition, there are two general information services which attempt to cover the whole field of computer information. The National Computing Centre's Information Services have been noted under the specific topics but, to provide a summary, are repeated here. The work of enquiry answering is based upon six indexes: software (the National Computer Program Index), hardware, background (*ie* company data), education, installations and literature. Several of these indexes are on the computer-based information retrieval system and others are being put on. Other information products from NCC include packages for KWIC/KWOC indexing and for thesaurus management, the

166

weekly *Computing journal abstracts,* the *NCC thesaurus of computing terms,* a numerical classification scheme and a number of other publications.

The Computer Information Centre Ltd (CIC) has also been mentioned previously on a number of occasions. This privately-run organisation operates an enquiry answering service to subscribers on all aspects of computing. Data is collected by means of press releases and brochures and checked back with the source as necessary. A monthly information bulletin is published and subscribers can obtain information by checking the short abstract provided. Private study facilities are available at CIC's offices. CIC also undertakes market research studies and operates a consultancy and programming service for visible record computers.

The Aslib Computer Information Group, although not an information service in the same way as the above two organisations, should be mentioned at this point. The group was formed in 1971 and is the first association in the field of computer information. It is concerned with the problems of the transfer of all types of information within the computer industry.

Unlike other industries, computing has been uninfluenced by the facts outlined in chapter 2, and this group of librarians, information officers and computer professionals has started the work of improving information transfer and of making the industry aware of the value of information. A number of meetings and an annual conference have been held. There are also working parties on topics such as classification and indexing, library aids, education, economic statistics and user needs.

The largest computer libraries in the UK are those of the two major manufacturers in the country: IBM and ICL, both of whom have a number of libraries.

ICL has its main library at the head office in London, which co-ordinates its other libraries at Stevenage (primarily engineering), Kidsgrove and Bracknell (both programming), Old Winsor (education) and some smaller libraries.

IBM's main libraries are at Croydon for IBM Ltd generally,

167

and this library controls smaller libraries and literature distribution centres in the regions; Hursley for the IBM (UK) Laboratories, which is the British agent for the ITIRC system and is more technically orientated than Croydon; Havant for IBM Information Services; Greenford—IBM Education Centre; Peterlee—IBM Scientific Centre.

Other computer firms with libraries are Honeywell, Elliott-Automation, AEI Automation, Ferranti and Control Data Ltd. NCR have unfortunately virtually closed their very good library.

Universities and research bodies with particularly notable libraries are the several colleges within London University, as well as the Institute of Computer Science, Manchester and Edinburgh Regional Computer Centres, Newcastle University, the Atlas Computer Laboratory at Didcot and Cambridge University. Most universities have a computer department, but there are not many other large libraries for these departments. In most cases the main university library contains the computer information.

The British Computer Society library is housed at the City University in London. It offers a loan service to members of the BCS and carries out literature searches. Its total stock is about 2,500 books, reports and pamphlets and it takes about 120 periodicals. The library is particularly strong on historical material and foreign periodicals. It is to be regretted that the BCS have recently cut back on library finances.

A number of software houses and other service organisations have libraries, although the recession in 1971 caused a halt in the expansion in this area. Some notable ones are those of Computer Analysts and Programmers, Unilever Computing Services Ltd and Scientific Control Systems.

Many large users of computers have specialist computer libraries, *eg* ICI (Mathematics and Computer Department, and Central Management Services), Eastern Gas Board, Mobil Oil, etc.

Finally, sections of the national library system such as the NLL and the National Reference Library have particularly good computer sections. The latter, especially, has improved its holdings greatly in the past few years and has much valuable material, *eg* a virtually complete set of all Auerbach publications.

There are no national information services in the US that are comparable with the NCC or CIC, although the Center for Computer Science and Technology of the National Bureau of Standards acts as a clearinghouse for computer information.

There are, however, probably well over a hundred computer libraries and specialist information centres attached to manufacturers (*eg* Burroughs, Honeywell, NCR and Univac), universities (Illinois, Texas, UCLA, MIT), research organisations (*eg* Mitre Corporation, Rand Corporation, System Development Corporation, and Battelle Memorial Institute), users of computers and computer services organisations (the Auerbach Corporation has an especially important one).

IBM has at least twenty four libraries of various types. The majority of these are linked with the ITIRC system, which has major branches on the West Coast, in England, and at La Gaude (France). ITIRC is a computer based information retrieval system which employs mainly natural language searching of abstracts of IBM and non-IBM generated literature. Printed bulletins are produced and an SDI service operated as well as normal batch searches. Most documents added to the system are available throughout IBM on microfiche. Descriptions have appeared in a number of places—the best one is still C A Merritt and P J Nelson, ' The engineer-scientist and an information retrieval system ', *Proceedings of the 1966 spring joint computer conference*, 205-212.

The ACM have, unfortunately, closed down their library and information service and little seems to be done at a national level by the major societies in the US, with the exception of Simulation Councils Inc. The ACM Special Interest Groups and Committees frequently publish bibliographies in their journals, but this is not really the formal information service which a body of ACM's standing should be offering.

Simulation Councils Inc offer a formal service in the area of simulation through SARE, a library service for reports, programs and other material on analog, digital and hybrid simulation. A bi-monthly bibliography is distributed and each subscriber receives, free of charge, up to 500 pages of reports that he wants, and also papers distributed at SCI regional meetings.

EUROPE

On the continent of Europe, the best library is that of the Studiecentrum voor Informatica, Amsterdam, which has a large collection of books, pamphlets, reports and periodicals. Its main interest is business data processing, and its collection is particularly strong on European literature. It offers a loan and photocopy service and publishes bibliographies. *Literature on automation* and the *International computer bibliography* are, in effect, an accessions list and a catalog respectively; not entirely so since both include abstracts from other organisations, but most items in them are Studiecentrum ones.

The International Computation Centre in Rome has a library as do the major manufacturers in Europe (*eg* Siemens, Telefunken, A/S Regnecentralen, IBM, Philips etc). Research centres such as IRIA near Paris and the Deutsches Rechenzentrum, Darmstadt also have good libraries.

Following the recommendations of a subcommittee of the Aigrain Committee which was formed by the European Economic Community to advise on European science and technology, there is to be set up a European Computer Information Centre. The precise organisational structure has yet to be decided, but it seems probable that it will be primarily a co-ordinating body, switching information between national centres who may well specialise in a particular topic as well as collecting all national information. The initial main area of interest is likely to be in program information.

170

SOCIETIES AND ORGANISATIONS

It has been indicated above that societies in the computer industry are not particularly aware of their formal information responsibilities if support of library/information units are an indication. They are, however, useful in putting enquirers in touch with specialists, since nearly all have a complex network of special interest groups. The ACM and BCS particularly operate in this way.

Other, non-computer societies and organisations also are of use to the person seeking computer information where specialist knowledge is required about computer applications, *eg* one would tend to approach the Royal Institution of Chartered Surveyors rather than BCS for information on applications in quantity surveying. On the other hand both BCS and Aslib have groups on applications in IR and libraries. To this end, therefore, in the next section some fairly general directories appear.

CONTROL OF LIBRARIES AND ORGANISATIONS

The tools for tracing the existence of libraries, societies, organisations and other information services have, in common with many other guides, grown considerably over the past few years. In view of this, and of the fact that there exists an excellent bibliography of such works: A P Harvey: *Directory of scientific directories* (Francis Hodgson Ltd), the following list is very selective:

The Aslib Computer Information Group should have published a combined directory of computer libraries and membership list, while for libraries generally there is the *Aslib directory* (third edition, 1968 and 1971), which covers science and technology in one volume and all other subjects in the other. Libraries are arranged geographically and details of stock and subject interest given. There are subject and organisation indexes.

The *Directory of British associations* (CBD Research, third edition, 1971) includes about 8,000 national and local societies and associations, while its companion *Councils, committees and boards* (1970) covers advisory committees, statutory boards,

171

councils, etc. Both works are well indexed and authoritative. The same publishers also are issuing the *Directory of European associations*. The first volume (1971) covers national industrial, trade and professional associations.

Another UK directory is P Millard *Trade associations and professional bodies of the United Kingdom* (Pergamon, fifth edition, 1971).

Research activities are covered by the annual *Scientific research in British universities and colleges* (HMSO), which appears in three volumes, and lists individual research projects in the physical, biological and social sciences. The latter volume also includes government departments. *Industrial research in Britain* (Francis Hodgson Ltd) lists government organisations, universities, firms and other bodies which offer research facilities, together with all services which back up research (including computing, abstracts and periodicals).

The UK is also included in the *European research index* (two volumes, second edition, Francis Hodgson Ltd), which covers government and independent research establishments, university research departments and research laboratories of industrial firms in thirty European countries (including eight East European ones).

The USA (as usual) is covered by a large number of services. The most useful library directory is A T Kruzas *The directory of special libraries and information centers* (Gale Research, second edition, 1968), which lists and indexes over 13,000 US and Canadian libraries, giving brief details of staff and stocks. A second volume comprises a geographic and personnel index. Other useful guides are National Referral Center: *Directory of information sources in the United States: physical sciences, engineering* (Library of Congress, 1971), which includes nearly 3,000 organisations; A T Kruzas: *Encyclopedia of information systems and services* (1971), which is a biennial guide to more than 800 information centres, networks, data banks and information storage and retrieval systems; and L Cohan *Directory of computerized information in science and technology* (Science

172

Associates/International), which lists machine readable data bases.

Associations are listed in the very comprehensive *Encyclopedia of associations* (Gale Research, fifth edition, 1967), which covers some 13,600 bodies in three volumes: main directory, geographic and executive index and new associations. There is also a keyword index which is cumulated. Another directory is *Scientific and technical societies of the United States* (National Academy of Science). Research activities appear in *Industrial research laboratories of the United States* (Bowker, thirteenth edition, 1970), which includes 5,327 laboratories in 3,115 organisations, with subject personnel and geographic indexes, and in *Research centers directory* (Gale Research, fourth edition, 1971), which includes 5,500 nonprofit research laboratories and is updated quarterly.

International guides include the previously noted *European research index* and *Directory of European associations; Guide to European sources of technical information* (Hodgson, third edition, 1970), which was previously published by OECD; the *World guide to libraries* (Bawker, third edition, 1971), which has details of 35,000 libraries in 157 countries, subject and geographical indexes and a very useful bibliography of other directories; and the *Yearbook of international associations* (Union of International Associations, annual).

26 LIBRARY AND UNION CATALOGS

HAVING ONCE TRACED a publication from the various services described in the previous chapters, the problem that then arises is how to obtain a copy of the item in question. In some cases there is little problem, since the abstracting service itself (*eg* *Dissertation abstracts* or GRA) is responsible for the distribution of the material contained in it. In addition, the National Lending Library for Science and Technology (NLL) is able to supply on microfiche all reports appearing in GRA, to lend many other reports (*eg* those of the Rand Corporation), to lend books (especially those in Russian), and to lend issues of about 28,000 serial titles. The National Reference Library in London has about 10,000 serial titles, a collection of early PB and AD reports and of AEC reports, as well as a collection of books and patents. All this, of course, presupposes that the material required is not available to the enquirer at his own library or locally.

In order to trace which library has a copy of any computer periodical, first source to check is the *World list of computer periodicals* (NCC, 1971). This includes holdings of 50 UK libraries, including detailed holding dates of the Nation Lending Library. This publication is to be revised and a new edition published in 1973.

The NLL itself has published *Current serials received by the NLL*—the third edition of which (1971) includes nearly 36,000 serials. These are mostly in science and technology, but there are significant holdings in medicine, management and the social sciences.

The National Reference Library publishes its periodical lists in three volumes: non-Slavonic titles in the Bayswater Division (1969), Slavonic and East European titles in the Bayswater

Division (1971) and current titles in the Holborn Division (1970). Nearly 25,000 titles are included and computer periodicals will appear in all three volumes.

Unless it is very recent, it is unlikely that a computer periodical cannot be traced in the above. If this should happen, however, then there are two other major union catalogs which can usefully be searched.

The *World list of scientific periodicals published in the years 1900-1960* (fourth edition, four volumes 1963-1965) contains about 60,000 periodicals held in 100-150 major and specialist libraries in the UK. It aimed to include all scientific periodicals, even if not held in a library anywhere in the UK. The *British union catalog of periodicals* (BUCOP) (five volumes 1955-1962) lists the holdings of over 500 libraries, and includes about 150,000 periodicals (including scientific ones). The two services have merged, and now publications are listed quarterly with annual cumulations. The arrangement is alphabetical by title with an organisation index.

These large national catalogs must necessarily be selective, both in the number of libraries who report holdings, and in holdings that they report. There are in existence, therefore, a number of local union catalogs for various areas published by the Library Association and by the cooperative schemes in the various areas.

Similar publications exist for many other countries. The USA has the *Union list of serials in libraries in the United States and Canada* (third edition 1966) and *New serial titles* (Library of Congress, 1953-). In addition, the Library of Congress publishes a union catalog of books—the *National union catalog,* which exists in both author and subject form. Although much of the publication of the NUC and its predecessors is outside the computer period (*ie* broadly, post 1945), it is worthwhile listing them in full, since they are extremely good examples of the fact that sheer size need not preclude rapid publication of union catalogs. Later issues are, in any case, important reference tools, since the NUC includes holdings of the Library of Congress and 400 other US and Canadian libraries. The chain of catalogs runs from 1901, as follows:

a) Author listings:

i) *A catalog of books represented by Library of Congress printed cards issued to July 31 1942*, 167 volumes.

ii) *Supplement . . . cards issued August 1 1942 - December 13 1947*, forty two volumes.

iii) *The Library of Congress author catalog 1948-1952*, twenty four volumes.

iv) *National union catalog: a cumulative author list* (1953-). A monthly periodical with quarterly, annual and quinquennial cumulations.

b) Subject listings:

i) *Library of Congress subject catalog* (1950-1952).

ii) *Library of Congress catalog. Books: subjects* (1953-). A quarterly periodical with annual cumulations which has also been published as quinquennial cumulations covering 1950-1964 in sixty seven volumes.

In addition, a card edition of the *National union catalog* (pre 1956 imprints) is being printed in book form—involving the duplication of over 10,000,000 cards on sheets.

The other important US library catalog is that of the Engineering Societies Library, which is a joint library for a number of societies (including the IEEE). The catalog, which appeared in thirteen volumes in 1963, contains 239,000 cards arranged by UDC with an author index. The coverage is of books, pamphlets, reports and bulletins. There are also supplements.

It should not be forgotten that the *International computer bibliography* is broadly speaking a catalog of the NAIPRC. In addition, many libraries in the field issue catalogs of their holding which, although not widely available, may be sent if requested.

APPENDIX

Code for Countries: AU Austria; BE Belgium; CZ Czechoslovakia;
DE German Democratic Republic; DN Denmark; DU Holland;
DW German Federal Republic; FR France; HN Hungary; IT Italy;
JA Japan; JU Jugoslavia; PL Poland; RM Roumania; RU USSR; SW
Switzerland; UK United Kingdom; US United States of America.
Periodicals marked * are translations from the Russian.

Rank	Periodicals	No of refs	Country
1	IBM technical disclosures bulletin	191	US
2	Communications of the ACM	148	US
3	IEEE transactions on computers	135	US
4	Tekhnicheskaya kibernetika	107	RU
5	Avtomatika i telemekhanika	106	RU
6	Engineering cybernetics*	105	US
7	Operations research	96	US
8	Automation and remote control*	95	US
9	Datamation	86	US
10	Technical cybernetics*	78	US
11	Proceedings of the IEEE	76	US
12	Computer journal	75	UK
12	Computer yearbook and directory	75	US
14	Data processing magazine	74	US
15	Kibernetika	73	RU
16	Fall joint computer conference	69	US
17	Computer report	66	JA
17	Data and control systems	66	UK
19	ACM national conference	64	US
19	Numerische mathematik	64	DW
21	Avtomatika i vychislitel'naya tekhnika	63	RU
21	Mathematics of computation	63	US

Rank	Periodicals	No of refs	Country
23	Computers and automation	62	US
24	Automatisme	60	FR
25	Bürotechnik + automation	59	DW
25	Computer design	59	US
25	Mechanizace automatizace administrativy	59	CZ
25	Simulation	59	US
29	Electronics	58	US
29	Journal of data management	58	US
29	Management science	58	US
32	Journal of the ACM	55	US
33	Electronic design	53	US
34	Data processing	52	UK
34	IEEE international conference record	52	US
36	Elektronische datenverarbeitung	50	DW
37	Computer bulletin	49	UK
38	IBM nachrichten	48	DW
38	IEEE transactions on information theory	48	US
38	IEEE transactions on magnetics	48	US
41	Business automation	46	US
41	SIAM journal of applied mathematics	46	US
43	Data processing (DPMA conference)	45	US
43	Standard EDP reports (Auerbach)	45	US
45	Automatizace	43	CZ
45	IEEE transactions on automatic control	43	US
45	Spring joint computer conference	43	US
48	Proceedings of the IEE	41	UK
49	Automatika	39	JU
49	Kybernetika	39	CZ
51	Economic computation and economic cybernetics	38	RM
51	Electronic engineering	38	UK
51	SIAM journal of numerical analysis	38	US
54	Izvestiya VUZ priborostroenie	37	RU

Rank	Periodicals	No of refs	Country
54	Journal institution of electronic and communications engineers Japan	37	JA
54	National electronics conference	37	US
57	Izvestiya Leningradskii elektrotekhnicheskii in-ta	36	RU
57	Mekhanizatsiya i avtomatizatsiya upravleniya	36	RU
57	Office automation	36	US
60	BIT	35	DN
60	Control	35	UK
60	Doklady akademiya nauk SSSR	35	RU
60	Messen steuern regeln	35	DE
64	Avtomatyka	34	RU
64	Computer	34	JA
64	Electronics letters	34	UK
67	Computer weekly	33	UK
67	Handbuch der mashinellen datenverarbeitung	33	DW
67	Industrial data processing applications	33	US
70	Revue de la mecanographie	32	FR
70	Trudy Siberskogo fiziko—tekhnicheskogo in-ta pri Tomskom un-te	32	RU
72	ADL nachrichten	31	DW
72	Elektronische rechenanlagen	31	DW
72	IEEE transactions on power apparatus and systems	31	US
75	ADI proceedings	30	US
75	Control engineering	30	US
77	Banking automation	29	US
77	Computer applications service	29	US
77	Electronics and communication in Japan	29	US
77	IBM journal of research and development	29	US
81	Datentrager	28	DW

Rank	Periodicals	No of refs	Country
81	Nuclear instrumentation and methods	28	DU
83	ADP newsletter	27	US
83	Journal of symbolic logic	27	US
83	Meres es automatika	27	HN
83	Zhurnal vychislitel'noi matematiki i matematicheskoi fiziki	27	RU
87	Automatisierung	26	DW
87	Calcolo	26	IT
87	Computing	26	AU
87	Information and control	26	US
87	Nauchnye trudy Moskovskogo in-zhenerno—ekonomicheskogo in-ta	26	RU
92	Automation	25	US
92	Bell system technical journal	25	US
92	Computes rendues	25	FR
92	ICT data processing journal	25	UK
92	IEEE transactions on nuclear science	25	US
97	IEEE transactions on communication technology	24	US
97	Instruments and control systems	24	US
97	Journal of the Franklin Institute	24	US
97	Management accounting	24	US
97	Problemy peredachi informatsii	24	RU
97	Wescon record	24	US
104	Archiwum automatyki i telemechaniki	23	PL
104	Cybernetics and electronics on the railways	23	BE
104	Ekonomika i matematicheskie metody	23	RU
104	Electronics magazine	23	JA
104	Nauchno—tekhnicheskaya informat-siya	23	RU
104	Priborostroenie	23	RU
104	Trudy Leningradskogo inzhenerno-ekonomicheskogo in-ta	23	RU

Rank	Periodicals	No of refs	Country
111	Cybernetics*	22	US
111	Data report	22	DW
111	Journal of applied physics	22	US
111	Operational research quarterly	22	UK
111	Systems and procedures journal	22	US
116	Business week	21	US
116	Office methods and machines	21	UK
116	Pribory i sistemy avtomatiki	21	RU
116	Public automation	21	US
120	Electrotechnology	20	US
120	Industrielle organisation	20	SW
120	Informacio elektronika	20~	HN
120	ISA journal	20	US

SUMMARY OF THE REMAINING STATISTICS

Number of journals	Number of references each
4	19
8	18
11	17
6	16
12	15
10	14
16	13
8	12
18	11
16	10
17	9
31	8
30	7
56	6
60	5
97	4
129	3
253	2
710	1

It will be noted that in the first edition, 105 journals produce 75 % of the references, while the more complete data presented in this appendix indicates that approximately the same number of periodicals produces only 50 % of the references. To list 75 % would have required 327 journals.

INDEX

This index includes all authors, titles and institutions (including some publishers) mentioned or described in the text. In addition, all abbreviations are included with, usually, a reference to the full form. This applies particularly to abstracting journals. In a few cases, when the abbreviation is better known than the full form, the index enters under the abbreviation.

185

186

191

194